HERE, THERE ARE NO SARAHS

A Woman's Courageous Fight against the Nazis and Her Bittersweet Fulfillment of the American Dream

SONIA SHAINWALD ORBUCH
FRED ROSENBAUM

Here, There Are No Sarahs

RDR Books
1487 Glen Avenue
Muskegon, MI 49441
Phone: (510) 595-0595
Fax: (510) 228-0300
E-mail: read@rdrbooks.com
Website: www.rdrbooks.com

and

The Judah L. Magnes Museum
Berkeley, California

ISBN 978-1-57143-130-1
Library of Congress Control Number: 2008942832

Copyeditor: Richard Harris
Proofreaders: Megan Trank and Ari Phillips
Design: Eric Triantafillou
Cover photo of Sonia: photographer unknown
Author photos: Paul Orbuch

Distributed in Canada by
Scholarly Book Services,
127 Portland Street, 3rd Floor
Toronto, Ontario, Canada M5V 2N4

Distributed in the United Kingdom and Europe by
Roundhouse Publishing Ltd.,
Atlantic Suite, Maritime House
Basin Road North,
Hove, East Sussex BN41 1WR
United Kingdom

Typeset in Chaparral Pro and DIN Mittelschrift
Printed in the United States

In memory of my parents, brothers, and husband—all of them fighters.

In gratitude to my son, Paul, for preserving our family's history.

SSO

Table of Contents

FOREWORD

OVER THE PAST THIRTY YEARS I have read many a survivor's
memoir and listened to countless hours of Holocaust testimony.
I do so as an antidote to my study of the perpetrators who so
much sought to dehumanize their victims that they were robbed
of all the elements of a personal narrative. "Your name is your
number" is the way one survivor put it. The Nazi murder machine
hoped that no Jew would survive, no witness would emerge, no
record would remain, and that the victims would stay nameless
and faceless forever. Little could they imagine how deeply, dare
one say obsessively, Jews were committed to historical memory,
to what ends they would go to record their memories in diaries,
letters, historical works, and, from the very first days after liberation, memoirs. No one could imagine that video documentation
centers would be developed precisely at a time when survivors
had reestablished their lives, raised their children and established their careers, and were prepared look back from a vantage

point of safety to speak to the world. The collective efforts of all the victims, the "drowned and the saved," remind us that there are six million personal stories, and each narrative of death, destruction, endurance, and survival has power and poignancy all its own. Only by joining one story with another, hearing each of these narratives, can we begin to understand the scope of an event we call by one name, the "Holocaust," which unfolded over twelve years in more than 20 different countries.

Here, There Are No Sarahs is especially salient because it deals with the little known phenomenon of Jews who fought back. Many works on resistance have been published in Hebrew because Israelis, especially in the first generation after the Holocaust, were looking for a usable history, one that could service their narrative of the heroic Jew and offer a model to the new Jew. Too few of these books have been translated into English. Fewer still are the works of women partisans who spent their war years in the woods.

Sonia truthfully explores the difficult role of women in resistance, particularly in the forests where they were subject to rape and exploitation, often considered the just rewards for the men who blew up trains or ambushed better-armed soldiers. Because she was protected, she was not injured and perhaps therefore more willing to speak, so we must appreciate the special character of this account.

Sonia was born and raised in the nurturing environment of Luboml, a classic shtetl. Growing up in a religious home, her life was marked by Sabbaths and holidays, family and tradition.

Historians distinguish between "perpetrators' time" and "victims' time." The Holocaust had its milestones—policy formulations, decisions, conferences, invasions, laws, decrees, boycotts, and battles—but that is not necessarily how the event was experienced by its victims. Suraleh (she would receive the name

Sonia later, in the partisans) knew very little of the overall Nazi plan or how Nazism permeated the climate of the 1930s, but she was not spared its venom. Although Poland had been the home of her family for generations, she was tormented by the refrain, "Jews go to Palestine." "Worst of all," she writes, "the authorities did not protect us."

In the beginning of this memoir she preserves her vantage point as a child. The outbreak of World War II is described in the way it impacted a fourteen-year-old girl about to begin her high school studies on September 1, 1939: "I never attended the *gimnazjum*."

In June 1941, the Germans invaded the Soviet Union, and Suraleh comments astutely on the response of the local population to the desperate conditions of the Jews. "The Nazis could not have been able to confine, enslave and ultimately annihilate the Jews of Eastern Europe had it not been for the willing help of locals." We now know a lot more about that enthusiasm. Recently gathered evidence from the killing fields of the Ukraine demonstrates that in many villages, it was not the Germans who slaughtered the Jews, but locals, so that they, and not the Germans, could expropriate Jewish property.

And yet, throughout this book, we also see another side of the Ukrainians. When the family flees to the woods, they meet a middle-aged Ukrainian peasant. Tichon Martynetz, at great risk to his life and seeking no reward, provides them the food, guidance, shelter, vital information, and even the human companionship necessary for survival. We do not know his motivation, but the narrator conveys the majesty of his character, how deeply, how totally, he dissents from the murderous policies of the Nazis.

But Suraleh's story is more than ghettoization, more than life in hiding. Together with her father and mother and her much-valued Uncle Hershel, a former scout in the Polish army, she joins the partisans and begins to fight back against the Germans. The nom de guerre she is given is Sonia, which she has carried throughout her life. Sura or Suraleh would have been too Jewish, too problematic.

Sonia served the traditionally female functions in the camp as a doctor's aide and kitchen helper, but she also participated in attacking German trains by planting mines and blowing up tracks. Unlike the prevalent perception, Jews fought in ghettos and in the forest, in mixed partisan units and also in exclusively Jewish partisan bands such as the famed Bielski Brigade that saved Jewish lives, sheltering Jewish women, children, and the elderly even as it fought the Germans.

Armed resistance was not the initial instinct of Jews. History had taught them the tools of spiritual defiance. Armed resistance occurred when Jews realized they were going to die and chose how to live in the time they had left. Fortunately, Sonia, her parents, and her uncle could hide because of the topography of northwestern Ukraine, where large, dense forests were situated near the ghettos. Sonia does not dwell on her role as a fighter but shares the conditions under which she and her family lived, and these descriptions of daily life in the partisans are among the most valuable recollections in this memoir.

There is a telling question about the credibility of a survivor's story: Does it sometimes make the reader uncomfortable with its honesty? Sonia expresses such candor about her relationship with the man who became her husband, Isaak Orbuch. She freely admits that he hadn't touched her soul the way another love had. Ten years Isaak's junior, she marries him for safety and security and reveals: "I wasn't sure I could let the opportunity slip away." The couple eventually make their way from Poland to the American zone and to the displaced persons (DP) camp. Sonia is again uncommonly frank regarding her family's black market activities. The reader should not pass too quickly over her description of Zeilsheim, the displaced persons camp that had a synagogue, yeshiva, sports clubs, and weddings every week soon followed by pregnancies and baby carriages. This was a miracle of Jewish history, the decision to respond to death by daring to bring new children into the world—Jewish children.

I was touched, too, by her description of life in Rego Park, Queens in the 1950s. I grew up in neighboring Kew Gardens and lived with survivors, who in those days were called refugees, *grineh,* the latest of the immigrants. My generation did not then appreciate the magnitude of their experience and its significance. My aunt and uncle were co-founders of the Orbuchs' synagogue, and I knew many of the people Sonia vividly describes.

She has found solace in looking back over her long life and bearing witness. Sonia, whom I know through her work with the Jewish Partisans Educational Foundation, and whom I admire for her strength and wisdom, lectures and teaches and has now written this poignant memoir. But this work is also the result of the fruitful and stimulating cooperation between a committed survivor and a skilled historian. I worked with Sonia's co-author, Fred Rosenbaum, on the *Encyclopaedia Judaica,* so I can attest to the quality of his writing. But here he was the midwife bringing forth the story from Sonia, insisting on specific details and historical facts. He kept his steady hand hidden so that it is Sonia's story we learn, Sonia's voice we hear.

A concluding word about evidence for memoirs: It is a truism that the earlier the testimony, the more it offers the scholar and the reader the raw material for historical writing. Personal memory dims over time, and what we have learned in the interim reshapes our conception of that time and that place. Yet the personal letters the reader will find in the appendix of this volume, written immediately after the war *but discovered by the authors only as they were completing their manuscript,* stand as a striking confirmation of Sonia's story. The letters of 1946 and 1947 hardly vary at all from the narrative told by a courageous and remarkably lucid woman sixty years later. As Sonia Orbuch has written, "The images are before my eyes now as they were then."

Michael Berenbaum
Los Angeles, California

PROLOGUE
German-Occupied Luboml, October 1942

THE UKRAINIAN POLICEMAN POINTED HIS rifle at my mother and me. He ordered us to lie face down in the gutter. "What will you gain by killing us?" she pleaded in his language. On my stomach, I looked up and glimpsed him, a youth who had played soccer with my brother.

For two days armed Ukrainians had been hunting Jews in the ghetto and turning them over to the Germans for execution. On this moonless night, my parents and I, hungry and almost driven insane from thirst, had crawled from our wretched hiding place to the edge of town. We found the outermost road blocked by sentries.

"You told my husband you'd let us through," Mameh cried out, and I wondered if my father, who had gone across first, could see us in the darkness. Just minutes before he had stuffed "American dollars"—in reality a packet of worthless payroll receipts—into the youth's hands to buy our family's freedom. Now it seemed that the ruse hadn't worked.

My mother begged for our lives. She kissed his uniform, his hands, his boots. Then she offered up her wedding ring, which he quickly pocketed. He fired his gun—over our heads—and let us pass through the last barrier from the town to the countryside.

After reuniting with father, we ran across fields and pastures to my mother's village about twenty kilometers away. Then we fled into the forest.

We would eventually be taken in by a partisan brigade and given the opportunity to fight back, but through the brutal winter of 1942-43 we were on our own, stalked by the Germans, the Ukrainian militias, and the elements.

I had a long time to be alone with my thoughts. Seventeen years old, I wanted to record how my happy childhood had come to a sudden end, how we suffered in the ghetto, how we endured the frigid weather in the wilderness.

Once I took a pointed twig and dipped it in the charcoal left by a fire we had made. On a piece of white bark from a birch tree I began to write. I didn't get very far; I needed pen and paper. It would be late in my life and not as a teenager that I would set down my story. But the images are before my eyes now as they were then.

1 | COCOON OF LOVE

I THOUGHT IT WOULD NEVER END, the life I knew in Luboml. I was born there in 1925, and my childhood in the shtetl was the best time I've ever known.

There were thousands of shtetls across Eastern Europe before the war, and Luboml was typical: a close-knit rural town with a bustling, open-air market and a high proportion of Jews, most of them Orthodox. Many who grew up in that culture have portrayed it as backward, parochial, and stifling. I experienced it differently—as warm, open, and nurturing. I wanted to live there forever.

Above all, I felt a sense of belonging. Everybody knew everybody else and, just to be sure, people were often called by nicknames that reflected their occupation or ancestral village, their handicap or special talent. There was Simcha the Watchmaker and Chaimke the Water Carrier, Moishe the Blind Man and Yoel the Half-Crazy One. I had a cousin who sang such a moving Kol

The Great Synagogue of Luboml.

Nidre prayer every Yom Kippur he was known by all as Binyumen Kolnidrik.

But while you had little privacy in the shtetl, you gained the genuine care and concern of your townsfolk. The values instilled in me there about family, community, and education—about the very purpose of life—have stayed with me through all the turmoil I've lived through since. Wherever I've gone, I've taken Luboml with me.

Between the wars, Luboml was in Poland, in the province of Volhynia, populated largely by poor, uneducated Ukrainian peasants; it is in Ukraine today. But the forested, low-lying region also contained sizeable Jewish and Polish minorities and a sprinkling of German-speaking *Volksdeutsche*. By the 1930s, our town had roughly 7,000 souls, about 4,000 of them Jews, primarily artisans and merchants who lived near the marketplace and in the shadow of the Great Synagogue.

That massive stone structure was erected in the late seventeenth century both as a fortress and a house of worship. Its parapet and turrets could be seen for miles and heralded the strength and security of the Jewish community, which dated from the 1300s. Even non-Jews sometimes came for the colorful Simches

Torah celebration, when dozens of red and blue Torah covers, embroidered with gold and silver, were strung on wires along the inside walls of the vast sanctuary. The Great Synagogue was featured on a postage stamp issued by Luboml just after World War I, with the name of the town printed in four languages: Polish, Ukrainian, German, and Yiddish. We Jews thought of ourselves as distinct from the others, but also as a permanent thread in the multiethnic tapestry of the place. On national holidays Jewish children sang patriotic Polish anthems in the Great Synagogue.

Yet, even as a child, I noticed suspicion and sometimes hostility among the Jews, Ukrainians, and Poles, and the climate of hatred worsened through the years. I also knew there had been massacres of Jews over the centuries. But I had little contact with non-Jews and felt protected. My life revolved around my parents, my two older brothers, my large extended family, and my friends at school, all Jewish. That was my Luboml.

So how could I have had even the faintest notion that the Jewish population and its six-century-long civilization would be destroyed overnight? Yet more than 99 percent of Luboml's Jews were murdered by the Germans and their local henchmen, and today not one Jew lives in the town. The Great Synagogue was used as a stable by the Nazis and later demolished by the Soviets. A parking lot now occupies the site. Nothing remains of the pulsating Jewish life of my town, nothing but memories.

We lived at 37 Chelmska Street, and up and down that major artery were the homes of my father's brothers and sisters. I had more than sixty aunts, uncles, and cousins nearby and saw them all the time. As I look back, I see my house, one of the nicest of our whole clan, thanks to my mother's resourcefulness and good taste. Born Beila Lachter, she stemmed from Nudyze, a tiny village in the environs of Luboml, but before her marriage she had lived in a mixed neighborhood in Warsaw for a couple of years, working as a milliner and gaining a bit of the big city perspective. Unlike most shtetl Jews in her generation, Mameh spoke Polish and Ukrainian with the same fluency as her native Yiddish.

She was an extraordinary homemaker, a *balaboosteh*, as we say in Yiddish, literally mistress of the house. Our wooden, two-bedroom, shingle-roofed house was not large, but everything about it was spotless and elegant. When you walked in you noticed the wooden floors, painted red and waxed to a high gloss shine. We were all required to walk on carpeted runners lest we leave scuff marks. God forbid if you strayed off the runner! The windows were decorated with Swiss tulle curtains, and mother designed and built a frame to wash and stretch them so that they always hung in perfect symmetry and looked starched. Extending almost the whole length of the dining room was a long table of blonde wood with a plush black leather sofa at each end. A grandfather clock stood against one wall; on another hung a painting of an English foxhunt.

The spacious master bedroom was bathed in light from its many tall windows. Cut velvet covered my parents' two beds, and on top of each was an enormous square pillow topped with more Swiss tulle. I slept on the opposite side of that room, in a smaller, matching bed with matching covers. My brothers had their own room and shared a big white enamel bed.

The house was filled with fragrant plants and flowers, and just outside mother's bedroom windows was her glorious little garden. It was admired throughout Luboml and sometimes my teachers asked if they could have some cuttings.

You may think that after seventy years I have embellished that house and garden, and no photograph exists for me to prove its charms, but my remembrance of it has never dimmed.

Every day, when we kids came back from school, Mameh served us dinner on a white linen tablecloth. I was such a finicky eater that she usually made me a separate meal, cooked in its own pot. To prepare for the Sabbath she awoke Fridays before dawn and baked delicious bread, challah, and cakes, which she stored in a built-in brick closet. All day the aromas of rising yeast, warm bread, and sugared batters would waft through the house. Mother even kept her own cow in a barn in our big backyard; she wanted to be sure that the milk we drank was fresh.

On top of everything else she was a magician when it came to fabric, able to fashion fine apparel for me from someone else's castoffs. She could take a shabby secondhand coat, turn it inside out, add a sporty collar and a row of buttons, and a lovely garment would emerge. And she made one article of clothing after another for my two fast-growing brothers. I can still see her now, sitting with us in the evenings, darning socks or stitching our garments on her tiny sewing machine.

She was no less meticulous about her own clothing and appearance. Her long, thick dark hair was worn in a single braid that she wound atop her head; it was exotic and alluring. On the high holidays she walked to the synagogue in splendor, dressed in an impeccably tailored black suit with a white jabot, or ruffled bib, and a matching hat trimmed in white ribbon.

True, for all of the refinements we enjoyed, we lacked indoor plumbing, refrigeration, or even running water. We cherished a gramophone, which we turned with a crank and played all the time, but had no telephone or radio. We read Yiddish and, occasionally, Polish newspapers, but to hear a broadcast of a breaking story we had to gather outside the open window of a neighbor who was fortunate enough to own one of the three or four radios in town. We got electricity in the late 1920s, but I can remember when we didn't even have that. Yet not knowing what I was missing, I never felt deprived. On the contrary, I relished the beauty and tranquility of my surroundings, and was grateful to my mother for the delightful world she created for me.

The summers, when I went on vacation in the countryside, were especially pleasant. Mameh arranged for me to stay with her mother in bucolic Nydyze. Bubbe Esther—a midwife and healer known as Esterka by the Ukrainian peasants, who all respected her—would take me by the hand for long walks through the dense forests. Together we'd pick succulent brown mushrooms and later grill them for supper. I loved the country air and the sound of the crickets, yet the sensation I recall most vividly was grandma's scratchy muslin sheets. Maybe that was because I was used to Mameh's linen, worn smooth and soft with washing.

Today Mameh might be called a "Supermom"—there was nothing domestic she couldn't do well. Often such perfection

My mother, Beila, on the right, with her sister Tziril.

leads to some sort of rebellion on the part of an adolescent girl, feeling inadequate, perhaps, and seeking to assert her own independent identity. There was much intergenerational conflict in Polish-Jewish families by the 1920s and '30s as both girls and boys chafed under age-old customs. But I was no rebel. I remained Mameh's perfectly behaved daughter up to the end, rarely questioning, much less disputing her judgment or authority. Her love and approval, and that of my father, was all I ever wanted.

Perhaps that was because I was slow to emerge from childhood even as I explored exciting new worlds through the many books I devoured. I was slight of build and ill a lot of the time with coughing fits, shortness of breath, fatigue, and high fevers and had to be taken to a specialist in Chelm, across the Bug

*My maternal grandmother Esther and my great-uncle,
the* melamed *Moishe Shneyers Povroshnik.*

9

River. Often my condition kept me indoors and alone when I longed to be in school or playing with my cousins. I was so sickly that our family doctor in Luboml, a kind man named Edward Amshchibovsky, would come in and check on me when he was in the neighborhood, whether I was suffering a bout of disease or not.

And I went through puberty late. I had my first period in 1939, at the age of fourteen, and then, perhaps due to my other physical problems, stopped menstruating. The monthly sign that a girl had become a woman would not return for many years.

I felt the normal stirrings of sexual desire as a teenager, but of course in Orthodox Jewish circles modesty and discretion prevailed. Sex was not discussed at home, and obviously we were not exposed to lewd images or erotic music in the mass media. My female cousins and I giggled when we saw couples walking hand in hand in a park, but we never talked about what they might be doing in private. The one and only time a boy carried my books home from school, I felt ashamed and confused—and terrified that we'd be seen. I was nearly twenty before I was kissed by a boy, and that was long after I'd left Luboml.

Not only was I innocent and sheltered, I was also spoiled. Being the youngest child, the only girl, and chronically ill, the whole family doted on me. My brothers chopped wood for the oven and carried heavy pails of water into the house. But did I help mother with her household duties? Not really. Mameh had everything ready for me before I went off to school in the morning. Every day she ironed all our clothes, including my pleated skirt, with a heavy coal-fired iron that sometimes gave her a headache. She prepared our lunches and served our breakfasts. My only chores, even as a teenager, were dusting the grandfather clock and the leaves of the plants on Friday afternoon. Otherwise I was just supposed to focus on my education. I was never sent to the market to buy food, and I never even learned to cook; maybe my folks thought the physical exertion would be too much for me or that there would be time for these things when I got older. Other girls sometimes stayed home on Friday to help their mothers prepare for Shabbes; my parents wouldn't even consider that. I was a Jewish Princess generations before the term was invented.

My gentle father pampered me, too; I was his favorite. How proud I was on Simches Torah when I'd hold aloft a little cardboard flag, its pole topped with a red apple and a candle stuck in that, and we'd walk hand-in-hand to the Great Synagogue. Wolf Shainwald, tall and good-looking, was brought together with mother by an arranged marriage. They both came from traditional families of eight children. Although they rarely displayed any outward signs of affection—few in their generation did—I could tell it was an excellent match. Their devotion to one another and to us kids was boundless. Father was always admired by my numerous aunts and uncles and by Jews throughout Luboml. In 1936, he was elected to the governing board of the Kehilla, the powerful umbrella organization of the Jewish community.

Like many in timber-rich Volhynia, he worked in the lumber industry, and he was quite successful before the Depression. During the week he'd travel to outlying villages and estates, negotiate for a concession to cut down trees, and then arrange to have the logs hauled on horse-drawn wagons back to Luboml. There the wood was cut in a sawmill and shipped by barge on the nearby Bug River to points near and far. Meanwhile, my brothers, while still schoolboys, started a little business of their own, which was very popular with the peasants. Using the leftover scraps of wood in our barn, they assembled crates, specially designed for the transport of poultry.

With all the lumber around, father lent boards to his many

My father, Wolf Shainwald, around the time of his marriage.

brothers and sisters and in-laws for the construction of their *sukkahs*, the outdoor booths in which observant Jews take their meals for the week-long festival every fall. He dutifully delivered and later picked up the wood. Yet sometimes Tateh, as I called him in Yiddish, failed to provide enough dry logs for mother to cook our Shabbes dinner on schedule; it threw off all her pains-taking planning and could bring her to tears. Those were the only times I would hear her rebuke him.

Often father's business trips kept him away from home during the week, but he'd always return before Friday night. He took the greatest pride in seeing our family sitting around the table and singing the joyous melodies. For Shabbes dinner Tateh usually brought home an *oyrech*, a poor person in need of a good meal. And once a week we offered an *esn tog*, or eating day, to help young yeshiva students so hungry and shy they barely looked up from their plates.

Father didn't have to tell me that aiding the needy was one of the most important mitzvahs, the word both for the command-ment and its fulfillment. I saw acts of loving kindness around me all the time. His mother, my Bubbe Gulleh, had her own special project: before every Shabbes she'd ask each of her neighbors to bake one small extra challah. These were for a destitute family with many children, and I vividly recall my tiny widowed grandmother, whom we thought of as ancient (although she was only in her sixties) garbed in an apron and wearing her sheitel, or traditional wig, going house to house to collect the little loaves before sunset. I regularly performed a good deed, too: every few weeks my parents sent me across town with provisions for an aunt and uncle not as fortunate as we were.

My family's charity did not revolve around food alone. Father was active in the *Chevrah Kadishah*, the Jewish burial society, and one of its main tasks was to help families who could not afford to give their loved ones a proper funeral. In our shtetl, as in most others, there were organizations to visit the sick, to provide interest-free loans to those starting businesses, to shelter transients, to offer Jewish learning to the children of the poor free of charge, and to pay the medical costs of the penniless. The Jewish community of Luboml was not wealthy but it did everything it could to take care of its own.

Father helped his fellow Jew and felt a deep connection to God in other ways as well. At sunrise he put on his *tallis* and *t'fillin* (his prayer shawl and phylacteries) and said his morning prayers; he made sure to bring his religious articles with him when he journeyed out of town. Although not a member of a Chasidic sect, something about the mystical movement touched his soul; he davened regularly at a modest, whitewashed Chasidic prayer house called a *shil'chl* (a little shul), which abutted the cavernous Great Synagogue but offered a much warmer environment. He was hardly an accomplished scholar but in the evening he delved into the holy texts, especially Pirke Avos, or Sayings of the Fathers, a compendium of ethical maxims. Our house was strictly kosher, and at home we observed the Sabbath regulations—we didn't haul water, light a fire, or even milk the cow; we hired a

Shabbes goy, a young gentile woman who performed those tasks for us.

Even Tateh's business could not be separated from his faith. Before signing a contract to lease a parcel of a forest, he would ask for the blessing of the rebbe, the spiritual leader of his Chasidic shil'chl, and then give the holy man a small percentage of the deal. He always took me with him for this ritual on Saturday evenings at the rebbe's home after an elaborate Havdalah ceremony marking the end of the Sabbath.

Yet Tateh was not as traditional as all that sounds. He was clean-shaven, and his *kapoteh*, the long black frock favored by ultra-Orthodox men, hung in his closet and was never worn. He preferred a sheepskin coat during the week and on Shabbes donned a fashionable western-style coat with fur lapels. Like my mother, he was fairly open to the modern ideas that affected Polish Jewry in the 1920s and '30s, and my parents' flexibility no doubt reduced any tension that might have arisen between them and their children.

His two sons were respectful of our parents but literally took a different path than the older generation. They'd walk with him to the synagogue every Shabbes morning, go inside, but then quickly leave and spend the day socializing with their friends and participating in sports and clubs.

Like many Jews who grew up in interwar Poland, they had more passion for Zionism than Judaism and were preparing in mind and body to make *aliyah,* to immigrate to Palestine. In other shtetls Jewish nationalism was often bitterly denounced by the Chasidim and ultra-Orthodox who fervently believed that the Jews could return to the Promised Land only with the coming of the messiah and that it was blasphemous to force God's hand. But in Luboml for some reason there was little opposition to Zionism even among the most pious Jews. A consensus arose about creating a Jewish homeland, although disagreement about how best to accomplish that goal led to a profusion of competing Zionist organizations. I was too young to join, but my brothers belonged to the spirited left-wing youth group Hashomer Hatzair, which sponsored outings, songfests, and theatrical productions. They both spoke modern Hebrew well, having learned it at a progressive Jewish school they attended almost every day after public school hours were over.

Unfortunately, girls were not thought to need that sort of Hebrew education or serious Jewish learning of any kind, and while some did receive such training, I was not among them. I was taught Hebrew by a disagreeable *melamed*, a tutor my parents hired on a daily basis every summer, but I never gained fluency in the language or any facility in the classical texts that were so vital to my father. In this sense Luboml was behind the times. In fact, one school I briefly attended for Orthodox girls, part of a well-regarded movement throughout Eastern Europe called Bais Yakov, was actually closed down due to the opposition of some narrow-minded rabbis. My parents, for whom my general education was of the highest priority, could not overcome the prejudices of their time and send me to the same supplementary Hebrew school as my brothers. Nor did I go to shul on Shabbes like the males in our family. My mother and I attended services only on the major holidays and, of course, sat in the crowded female gallery upstairs, where one woman recited prayers and the rest of us repeated the verses in low tones. It was not my nature to voice any irritation, but inwardly I resented being excluded from the world of Jewish knowledge that only boys could enter.

Shneyer, born in 1918, was the older of my two brothers. Tall and blonde, he could have passed for a non-Jew. He was an avid soccer player and popular at school. But most of all I remember how decent he was: honest, caring, and generous to a fault. When

I was little, I'd climb up on his shoulders and try to beat him up. He didn't seem to mind. After I started school, he'd sometimes take me to class on his bike and when I forgot to bring my lunch, he'd cycle over and hand-deliver it. I was so pleased when friends saw my strapping big brother shower this attention on me that sometimes I purposely left my lunch at home. And then at the age of twelve, when I wanted to be in the school orchestra, it was Shneyer who bought me an instrument, a mandolin.

Sometimes Shneyer even took me on Shabbes eve to the one movie theater in town, which a friend of my father's had opened a few years after I was born. The first time I went, as a ten-year old in 1935, the main feature was preceded by a newsreel of the grand funeral in Warsaw of Poland's benevolent dictator, Marshal Josef Pilsudski. The camera scanned thousands of mourners in the streets of the capital. A woman sitting next to us evidently thought the screen was a big, brightly lit window onto the marketplace of Luboml, right outside the cinema, and murmured, "All these people in our little town, where are they going to spend the night?" Next on the bill was the *Count of Monte Cristo*, a romance not considered appropriate for children. Shneyer was afraid I might be spotted by one of my teachers, so I hid under my seat during the intermission. Our parents might have preferred a different Shabbes pastime for their kids, but they indulged us nonetheless. At least we didn't have to violate the Sabbath by paying admission; my family had a season subscription.

Meir, black-haired and three years younger than Shneyer, had a very different personality. He, too, revered our parents and was loyal to the family. But he also wanted to have a good time. Strikingly handsome, with lots of friends both male and female, he sported the trendiest clothes you could buy in Luboml and learned the latest steps to the tango and fox trot. Girls in his class, wanting to catch his eye, often came over to our house under some pretense. When they told us they needed to ask him the homework assignment, we'd nod knowingly.

"Meir Kesir," or Meir Caesar, as he was known, also enjoyed many hobbies, outlets for his creative energy. A talented woodworker, he once presented me with a masterfully crafted inlaid jewelry box. But some of his other pursuits struck us as eccentric. One year he raised half a dozen pigeons in our yard and built a little loft for them in their cages, complete with stepladders and swings, bridges and birdbaths. When he'd come home from school, he'd let out the flock, and kids from the neighborhood would descend on our house with sacks full of grain for the birds. It caused such a commotion that mother simply couldn't tolerate it anymore. One day, with Meir out of the house, Mameh released

My brother Meir Shainwald, second from the left, and his friends in Luboml.

17

the pigeons at an hour when she knew they'd become confused and never return. Just to be sure, she locked their empty cages. As soon as Meir came home and found them all gone, he was inconsolable. I don't know how serious he was when he threatened to drown himself in our well, but he had one leg over the side before mother could calm him down. They compromised by switching from pigeons to little chickens, and Meir built an even more elaborate coop for them—a small village for his feathered friends.

Only once did Meir cross the line and truly anger my father. For a brief while in the late 1930s, around his seventeenth birthday, my brother frequented a low-class bar that served non-kosher meat and catered to rowdy types, both Jews and non-Jews. People informed Tateh that they'd seen his son enter the disreputable establishment and hang out with hard-drinking laborers. One evening at dinner my mild-mannered father exploded. He slapped Meir hard across the face, shocking us all. Meir, I'm sure, was hurt less by the physical blow than the realization that he had disappointed our father. Humiliated, he got up immediately and went to the barn where he spent the night. I don't think either of them ever spoke of it again, but I know Meir dropped that circle of drinking buddies.

I, on the other hand, was the goody-goody. I was Sura then. (I would receive my Russian name, Sonia, only later.) Little Sura, or Suraleh, could do no wrong. At school I was at the head of the class, which pleased my parents no end. Some of the other kids teased me when they heard of the glowing reports my instructors sent home, but even that praise was less effusive than how my mother described me to the teachers: "When Sura comes in, she brings the sun with her." I was embarrassed by this florid prose, but only a little.

For the first few years I attended a public school, which had only Jewish children, about a mile away and above a firehouse. My generation of Jews was the first for which Polish was compulsory; I learned it well and speak it fluently to this day. A year before the war, when I was thirteen, I was selected for a newly built, well-appointed school for gifted kids including Ukrainians, Poles, and Jews and I thrived in that school as well. Among the many subjects we studied were the works of patriotic nineteenth-century Polish literary giants like the epic poet Adam Mickiewicz and the novelist Henryk Sienkiewicz. I never developed any great love for Poland, but I became engrossed in the legendary tales and admired the self-sacrifice of the heroes. Class was held six days a week including Saturdays, but at least the authorities were willing to bend a little: We Jewish youngsters weren't required to write in our notebooks on Shabbes; we could just sit back and listen to the lessons.

Amidst the contentment of those years was a dark side to the idyllic life my family led, yet few outside of the five of us were aware of it. With the Depression in the early '30s, my father's once-robust lumber company failed; he simply could no longer collect the sums owed him by his customers around the country. So he was forced to borrow money to cover his business debts and our household expenses, signing promissory notes called *wechsels* to private lenders.

 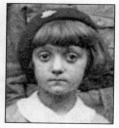

My elementary school class photo, early 1930s. Only four of us survived the war.

19

But he had great difficulty paying them back. The *prozent-nikes,* as the creditors were known, because they made a living by charging percentage points, had a bad reputation in Luboml, and one day I found out why. I was sitting in the kitchen, calmly sipping a cup of cocoa, when a loan shark who had come to collect his money banged his fist on the table and snarled in my direction: "You're drinking my blood!" I could never banish those words from my mind.

Another unwelcome visitor was the tax collector, who tended to prey on middle class Jews in particular. With no money to pay the levy, we knew they'd confiscate our furniture or valuables. When they came, we'd lock the door and hide, hoping that if they thought no one was home, they'd move on and afflict some other family.

My unemployed father, meanwhile, didn't know what to do with himself. Around forty years old and considered the crown prince of all the Shainwalds, he had to find another source of income. After much deliberation, he decided to lease a big electric-powered oil press and produce sunflower and flaxseed oil.

But luck was not with him and the venture ended in disaster. Without father's authorization, one of his employees, a man who struggled to support his family, entered the premises on Sunday and began work—in violation of Poland's strict Blue Laws, which mandated no business of any kind on the Christian Sabbath. He somehow got entangled in the moving parts of the machine and was crushed to death. After Tateh was informed of the accident he rushed over to the plant and, as soon as he reached the scene, fainted. He was quickly revived but had to be drenched with so much water that he was carried home dripping wet, his head and neck wrapped in a burlap sack to protect him from the winter cold. I was haunted by his strange appearance and horrified about what would follow. Fortunately no criminal charges were filed—the Polish authorities could easily have blamed him for the tragedy—but Tateh's short career as an oil producer and wholesaler was over.

His next attempt was another fiasco. Tobacco, grown domestically, was a tightly regulated and highly taxed government monopoly, so someone suggested buying some on the black market and selling it for a profit. Tateh borrowed a considerable amount of money from a favorite niece and rode to a nearby town for a clandestine meeting with a band of smugglers. My mother, brothers, and I were sickened to see Father, a pillar of the community, forced to go to such lengths to provide for us, and of course we also feared for his safety. But none of us felt any moral qualms about his going outside the law—the Polish state was out to ruin us economically, we believed, and it was not wrong to break its cruel and stupid rules.

Father returned with a huge load of contraband, seventy kilos, which we quickly concealed in an inconspicuous space between our house and barn. But our hearts sank as soon as we untied the sacks—they contained nothing but paper and stones! This endeavor wouldn't bring in one zloty, and of course father was on the hook for the loan. How he could have cut the deal without checking the merchandise I don't know. But none of us uttered a word of reproach; rather, we were overwhelmed with pity for Tateh. Somehow, he retained his dignity, but to see him suffer these financial reverses was the worst part of my childhood.

Now desperate for money, my parents rented out their splendid master bedroom, which had its own door to the street, to a non-Jewish policeman for twelve zlotys a month and charged him another three for the buttermilk he drank in the morning. We moved our beds to the kitchen. The cop turned out to be friendly and even invited me to spend Christmas eve with him and wife, who was visiting from their village, an invitation I was pleasantly surprised my folks let me accept. I helped them decorate the tree, and they fed me some luscious chocolates. But that was small consolation for losing our bedroom.

Mother also cooked dinner every evening for two teachers new to Luboml; she set them up at a separate table, away from our family. And she made sure the curtains were drawn; she didn't want her friends and relatives to know of our difficult circumstances.

But it was hard to keep up appearances as the Depression deepened. Mameh ran a tab with many storeowners, taking goods "on the book," as we termed it, but eventually ran out of credit and couldn't even obtain the proper food for our traditional Shabbes dinners. Sometimes neighbors would knock on our door Thursday evenings and remind her that the stores would soon be closing. But she never told them why she hadn't shopped; she made up some excuse and said she'd go to the market first thing in the morning. It wasn't only her own pride at stake; I think she feared if word got out that Wolf and Beila Shainwald were in need, it would demoralize the whole neighborhood in those hard times. Yet when no smoke came out of our chimney, it was obvious to all that there was no feast on our table.

A year or so before the war, as I entered my teens, things began to look up. Shneyer, around twenty and previously unable to find steady employment, went into the lumber business in partnership with my father's most prosperous brother, Uncle Tratl. At this time, too, my father regained a place in the industry. We were able to pay our bills, no longer needed our boarder, and finally felt a little better off.

But if the economy improved, the anti-Semitism never ebbed, and I became increasingly aware of the animosity toward the Jews. The first Polish republic had come into existence after the Treaty of Versailles following World War I, and the Poles, who had chafed under foreign rule for a century and a quarter before their independence, were now fiercely nationalistic. Relations between the Poles and the Ukrainians, Belorussians, Lithuanians, and ethnic Germans in their midst were difficult. But it seemed that Poland's three million Jews—who constituted 10 percent of the population by the late 1930s—were the most despised minority group. While Poland was threatened by Nazi Germany and Soviet Russia, politicians accused us of being disloyal, the Church branded us as Christ-killers, and the peasants suspected us of being dishonest.

Especially after the death of Marshal Pilsudski in 1935, we knew the government in Warsaw was our enemy. A year later, just to insult us, the Polish parliament, with a lot of fanfare, passed a series of laws phasing out kosher slaughtering as inhumane. At the same time, the leading Polish cardinal publicly labeled us atheists, Bolsheviks, usurers, pornographers, and pimps. Claiming we ran too many taverns, he even blamed us for Poland's alcoholism problem.

Attacks against Jews in the streets were now more common, and sometimes Meir came home with a bloody nose. He had been in fistfights with *Poznanchiks*, young Polish hooligans from the city of Posen who descended upon Luboml in the summers. They harassed the elderly along with the young, often pulling the beards on faces of Orthodox Jews. And the local teenagers could be sadistic as well. One Jewish boy we knew told us how his Ukrainian classmates held him down and pushed pork into his mouth.

Worst of all, the authorities did not protect us. I felt physically safe because girls were generally spared the physical violence of the kind my brothers encountered, and at the mixed school for advanced children that I attended in the late '30s most of the teachers were Jewish. But even there I was stunned one day at an assembly when the Polish principal addressed us with the most commonly heard slogan of the anti-Semites: *Zydi, l' Palestina,* "Yids, go to Palestine." He would repeat that slur many times.

Something had to be seriously wrong, I sensed, because I frequently heard mother urge Shneyer to immigrate to Argentina. His first choice would have been Palestine, but by the time he was old enough to go, in the mid-1930s, it was hard to obtain an entry permit. And it became nearly impossible after May 1939, when Britain issued its notorious White Paper virtually closing the gates of the Jewish homeland. The United States, of course, was inaccessible due to the meager immigration quotas set by Congress in 1924. South America remained an option, and mother's oldest brother had gone to Buenos Aires in the mid-1920s, and another sailed a decade later. But Shneyer would not consider leaving the family.

Yet, I lived in a dream world, largely oblivious to the mounting peril. On Shabbes afternoons I'd play with my cousins and overhear the adults talking of grave matters, but it made little impact. One aunt repeatedly told of how she'd hidden from a murderous Ukrainian gang just after World War I, when pogroms raged throughout Volhynia. She'd submerged herself in a lake and breathed through a long straw. "There she goes again," we kids would chuckle among ourselves, "The old folks sure love their war stories."

In the spring of 1939 I was thrilled with the news that I'd passed the rigorous series of exams for the *gimnazjum*, the only academic high school in Luboml. I was one of a select few chosen to study in depth the subjects I loved: literature, history, geography, and science. No one in my huge extended family had ever advanced that far scholastically. I did not harbor any hopes of going on to the university. A tiny fraction of Jews and females was afforded the opportunity for higher education, and I knew that finding a job after graduation would be next to impossible. But the gimnazjum, I thought, would be the perfect finishing school. Although I might never quite be the balaboosteh my mother was, I figured I'd be well educated.

But the private, nonsectarian high school, like its counterparts across the country, was frightfully expensive—50 zlotys a month, about half of what we spent on food for the whole family, and food was by far our major expense. I was wracked with guilt when I realized the hardship my parents would have to endure to set aside that kind of money. Of course my mother's fondest wish was for me to attend the gimnazjum, but she was also realistic and discussed an alternative: enrolling in the affordable, well-run ORT vocational school in Lvov, about a hundred kilometers away, and learning to be a seamstress. I felt torn between my own desires and the welfare of my family. Would it be right for me to ask them to sacrifice so much?

Then Shneyer stepped up and solved the dilemma. If he wasn't drafted into the army and could keep working, he said, he'd pay half the tuition (a significant part of his earnings as a novice lumber merchant, I'm sure). Then our parents would shoulder the other half, still a heavy burden but one they could carry.

I was immensely grateful and overjoyed. Mother sewed my navy-blue uniform and also made me a fine coat with a fur collar. I purchased my books and school supplies and couldn't wait for school to begin. Classes were scheduled to start the first week of September 1939.

2 | LOSING TRUST

I NEVER ATTENDED THE *GIMNAZJUM*. The war broke out on September 1, 1939, and bombs rained down on Luboml. A window in our house was shattered, and my life was turned upside down more than I could know.

Awakened around 4 a.m. by the explosions, I got out of bed and went outside just as Meir came bouncing up to the front door. He was returning from a late-night dance and wearing gleaming white pants. Uppermost in his mind was washing and ironing those trousers for another social event later in the day.

But the rest of us were not so easily distracted. There had been much tension leading up to that awful hour. Hitler had been menacing our country for a year, demanding the return of Danzig and the right to build a highway across the Polish Corridor, which separated the two parts of Germany. Only two weeks before the hostilities, he had signed a treaty with Stalin removing any Soviet threat to his eastern border.

Meir (second from left) out with friends.

My parents, who read the Yiddish newspapers, had to have been deeply concerned about these developments. But to me, a fourteen-year-old on summer vacation, with little interest in politics, and living in a house without a radio, the war came as a total shock. If I was vaguely aware of anything, it was the bombast of the Polish government. People mocked the nation's commander-in-chief, Marshal Rydz-Smigly, for his ridiculous prediction that in any conflict with Germany, no Polish soldier would lose so much as a button from his uniform.

In the late summer of 1939 I thought I knew what war was—large armies clashing on a distant battlefield. But then why was Luboml bombed? It had no military or industrial targets. And without a telephone, my family had no way of knowing if other towns had suffered the same fate. The next day all we had to go on were rumors and secondhand reports from people who had heard official broadcasts, mostly propaganda. Some big-city inhabitants were able to tune into BBC and other foreign news services, but this was not the case in our shtetl.

In the town square we learned by word of mouth of the persecution of Jews in Germany. It all seemed unreal to me. I was frightened and confused as a clouded future loomed ahead. But most of all I was upset that school was not starting. Like the other kids, I had to stay home.

To make matters worse, I soon became violently ill with typhoid fever I had probably caught on my recent visit to the countryside. I ran a very high fever, couldn't keep food down, and was so weak that I couldn't get out of bed. Medical care was hard to obtain in those chaotic weeks, but Dr. Amshchibowsky treated me and brought a few lemons, the only food for which I had any appetite. How he got them under such circumstances I'll never know.

Meanwhile, the Polish army, under-equipped and badly led, quickly collapsed, and in about two weeks gray-uniformed German patrols entered our town, followed by more troops. In light of what would happen later, it is astonishing that they did no one any harm at that point. They even distributed sweets to the children and bought postcards of the Great Synagogue. And they left within three days.

For the next twenty-one months we would be occupied not by the Nazis, but by the Soviets. The Red Army invaded Poland from the east on September 17, and a secret section of the Non-Aggression Pact, signed the month before, called for the two powers to divide Poland roughly in half. The border was to be the Bug River, fifteen kilometers west of Luboml, so we were safely within the Soviet zone. The Wehrmacht had gone too far and had to pull back.

Now the ground shook under the weight of the Soviet tanks. Red Army men swarmed in the main square. They even choked the streets as they marched to the communal baths together, filling the air with revolutionary ballads.

Still in my sickbed, I heard my parents and brothers speaking worriedly of what might be in store for us. Of course, my

Poland after the outbreak of World War II.

family was relieved not to have come under Nazi rule; even without an inkling of the Final Solution, we knew the Soviets were the lesser of two evils. But we were distressed anyway, because Stalinist brutality was familiar to us. Around 1930, when I was still a little girl, my older cousin Henya had married an idealistic young lawyer inspired by the writings of Marx and Lenin. The newlyweds decided to immigrate to the Soviet Union but were hardly welcomed with open arms. The Kremlin was suspicious of Polish Communists, and soon after their arrival he was arrested and tried for espionage. He received a twelve-year sentence at

A poster depicting a Soviet soldier killing an eagle, the Polish national symbol, and breaking the shackles of the peasants. (Courtesy of the Arthur Waldo Collection of the Hoover Institution, Stanford, California)

hard labor (he would die of pneumonia a year after his release) and Henya was assigned work in Kharkov, where she lived in misery and loneliness. So we had few illusions about the Red Army bringing freedom to Poland.

Everyone spoke of the invaders as *bourvasseh*, the barefoot ones. They wore boots, of course, but the term reflected the fear of a revolution being forced on us from abroad: barbarian hordes seizing all the property and redistributing it to the poor.

A good number of left wing Jews in Luboml, many of whom had sat in Polish prisons for their Communist activities, enthusiastically waved red flags, and, with some Ukrainian Communists, erected a victory arch to welcome the "liberators." This kind of behavior naturally enraged the Poles, in mourning for their republic, which was now in tatters only twenty years after its birth. During the interwar period many of them had wanted a Poland with no Jews; now they still had the Jews but no Poland.

Just before the arrival of the Soviets, some Polish soldiers, retreating through our town, killed a few Jewish men, and tore down the arch.

In fact, the embittered Poles would never forgive the Jews for what they saw as collaboration with the godless Bolsheviks. But even though some Jews served in the Soviet administration, the large majority of the Jewish population was victimized under Stalin's rule. I don't believe most Poles have ever understood that. Especially in Volhynia, the great majority of Jews were not leftists eager to settle a score, but rather Orthodox for whom Judaism was the centerpiece of their lives.

And the rich Jewish life we had known before the war was crushed at the outset of the occupation. The Great Synagogue, as well as the smaller shuls, ceased to function, and my father's minyan was forced to meet in a private home. Most Jewish communal institutions were likewise dismantled—even the old Jewish cemetery was desecrated—and Zionist organizations received particularly harsh treatment. Speaking Hebrew was prohibited. We were required to go to work and school on the Sabbath and Jewish holidays.

Jews were also hurt economically, in some ways even worse than the rest of the population. Many, like my own family, owned small businesses and lost their livelihoods with the abolition of free enterprise. Middle-class Jews were in a panic from the beginning; they hid their valuables and even donned drab, old clothes so as not to attract attention. Storekeepers were especially vulnerable. Probably in order to deter looting, the Soviet command issued every soldier hundreds of rubles, which, along with the zloty, were now declared legal tender. Shop owners were not allowed to raise prices, and Red Army men cleaned them out, buying every stick of merchandise on the shelves with money that soon became worthless due to runaway inflation. I heard of soldiers proudly wearing half a dozen wristwatches at once.

We were all struck by how crude and ignorant they were. Some even bought *tallesim* and unthinkingly wore the prayer shawls to keep warm. And once their families came to join them, several officers purchased nightgowns for their wives, who mistook them for evening dresses and wore them to parties. In another town a Soviet soldier reportedly bought a woman's bra and wore it as earmuffs. I heard one Russian claim, upon seeing oranges, that in his country they were plentiful because they were mass-produced in factories! It may well be that the Red infantry was coached before the invasion to mouth such lines so the local population would get the impression that the Soviet Union was a land of abundance. In reality, one of the most backward parts of Poland looked to them like the Garden of Eden.

My family was not amused. It was clear from the beginning that the residents of Luboml, a strategic spot near the new border, would have to quarter many Soviet troops. Within days the authorities turned over my parents' bedroom to a senior officer and his wife. The couple, Jews from Kiev, always acted properly towards us; our two "guests" cooked on a Primus stove and ate their meals by themselves. But now our family of five was squeezed into a kitchen, dining room, and living room. My parents divided the kitchen in two with a "Spanish wall," a partition that did not reach the ceiling, and slept there.

It was a big imposition, but much worse was the anxiety we all felt that Tateh could be sent away to Siberia. Early in the occupation a "plebiscite" had been held—an election filled with intimidation and rigged vote counts—and on that basis eastern Poland was incorporated into the Ukrainian Republic of the USSR and we became Soviet citizens. But the identity card my father was issued listed his occupation as "capitalist" and we had heard of other local entrepreneurs, including a well-known woman who owned a big fabric store, who were sent in sealed freight cars to labor camps in the frozen Russian interior. After the war I wasn't surprised to learn that about 75,000 civilians were deported from Volhynia during the Soviet occupation, and more than half a million from all of eastern Poland—almost 4 percent of the entire population. Jews accounted for about a third of those exiled, three times their proportion of the inhabitants.

Eventually Tateh was given a position of much responsibility, overseeing seventy workers at a state-run lumber mill, but we always dreaded that his past business ventures could brand him as an enemy of the people. Shneyer continued to work in the timber business, too, and Meir was assigned a decent job in a bread distribution center, where he received enough bread to trade or give away to others. Father was also able to barter wood and other supplies for food and clothing—and he could lay his hands on some boxes of soap and candy from Russia intended for the many laborers he supervised, so, given the chronic shortage of goods, we felt a little luckier than most. But no one in the family felt secure.

My life revolved around school once I regained my health. I missed the first few weeks, but Tateh, who had grown up when our part of Poland was under the Czars, bought some Soviet newspapers and used the time to teach me the Cyrillic alphabet and a bit of Russian. It was a good thing, too, because that was now the language of instruction. New Russian-speaking instructors were recruited, and the old teachers were expected to learn the new language in a crash course.

The academic quality was high—the best aspect of life under the Soviets—and I eagerly delved into my studies. Russian came quickly to me, and I got high marks during my two years in the system. In our school orchestra I played the mandolin, and my classmates and I were occasionally sent out of town to Olympiads (patriotic competitions among youngsters in sports, music, and dance) held in stadiums in Volhynia's larger cities. Best of all, the high school was free. My family would not have to suffer an economic hardship to give me a good education.

Polish was no longer taught—depolonization was a clear goal of the authorities—but, along with Russian and German, we studied Ukrainian, and even Yiddish because Stalin hoped to convert each ethnic group to communism through its own language. Yet it was an odd form of Yiddish they put up on the blackboard, an idiom shorn of its Hebrew roots. Such disdain did they have for the language of the Bible that they changed the spelling of those Yiddish words which are identical to Hebrew. *Emes,* for example, meaning truth in both languages, they spelled with the letter *ayin* instead of *aleph* to differentiate it from Hebrew. When my parents saw my homework we joked that the teachers wrote the word Noah with seven mistakes.

They tried to indoctrinate the younger children with atheism, the teenagers more with Soviet nationalism. My class was shown primitive films depicting the USSR as a "workers' paradise," but the tractors, collective farms, and superhuman factory workers known as Stakhanovites inspired no one. To my friends and me, communism seemed alien and offensive. It never made the slightest dent in our Jewish identity.

But when I was chosen to be a Pioneer Leader, the very first step toward becoming a party member, I was afraid to refuse. I knew if I declined the "honor" it might reflect badly on my father and put him in further jeopardy. So I wore the red kerchief they gave me, which stood out against my uniform of a black apron and white collar trimmed with lace. I performed my duties: taking the younger children on outings, counseling them in the playground, and handing out some propaganda.

A year later, though, in the fall of 1940, the stakes were a lot higher. Now fifteen, I was nominated for the Komsomol, the Communist youth group.

To this day I resent the person who recommended me, a boy my age from the poor side of town, whose working class folks had sided with the Reds before the war. He sat directly behind me in class and pulled my braids; maybe he had a crush on me. He submitted my name, probably thinking he was doing my family and me a big favor. "It will help you the rest of your life," he insisted, ignoring every signal I could give him that I'd rather not participate.

Before long he handed me a notice that left me trembling. I was to report to a committee that would decide whether or not I'd be admitted to the Komsomol. To refuse could make things even worse for my father than if I had turned down the Pioneer Leaders. But I really didn't want to join something so repugnant and contrary to everything I had learned at home.

How could I get them to reject me without compromising my family? If I appeared stupid, they'd know it was an act; I was one of the best students in my class. I had a host of childhood ailments, but I was afraid and embarrassed to use my bad health as an excuse. I went to my parents with my predicament, and I could see the worry it caused them, but they didn't try to coach me. They probably thought it would only add to the pressure I already felt.

Finally the day of my interview arrived, and after school I walked through the autumn leaves across town to the party headquarters, still unsure of what to do. I was so tense my legs could barely carry me.

I entered the building, and someone led me down a hallway to a meeting room. I opened the door and saw about half a dozen important-looking adults, men and women, some in uniform and some not, sitting behind a semicircular table. As I stood before them, they fired questions at me, and I was taken aback by their brusque tone:

"Is your father a bourgeois?"

No, I answered.

"But didn't he own the sawmill?"

No, I stated, he only rented it to cut wood.

"Then your brother was the owner."

No, I said, Shneyer had nothing, he was just starting out.

And so it went, for a full hour, with queries about everything from the heroics of the October Revolution to the infallibility of Comrade Stalin. I told them what I thought they wanted to hear even as I prayed they wouldn't accept me.

A few days later I received a letter congratulating me on becoming a Komsomol. Now I had to go to meetings, held in school before or after class, and listen to a never-ending barrage of propaganda about how good things were in the Soviet Union. And I was expected to convince my classmates of the same.

I felt I was leading a double life, ashamed of myself for being a turncoat to my family and friends, yet constantly dreading that the party officials would see that my heart wasn't in it. My greatest fear was that they would ask me to inform on someone—which undoubtedly would have happened if this regime had remained in place. I might have had to live a lie for the rest of my years.

The Communists endowed everything with utmost serious-ness. I had to see the pompous Luboml party secretary himself to pick up my Komsomol membership card, an elaborate docu-ment that looked like a passport. He solemnly told me that my ID number was top secret. If any unauthorized person learned it, the gravest consequences would follow.

For the next year I guarded it closely, my badge of dishonor, and slept with it under my pillow. To keep it safe during the day, my mother sewed a special pocket inside the blouse of my school uniform. My brothers and their friends sometimes joked that they'd peeked at the card, found out the secret number, and would spread it around the school. I wasn't completely sure they were kidding, and I don't think they realized how upset they made me.

In those days, it appeared that everyone suspected everyone else of treason. Before the war the lines were clearer—the world seemed divided between Jew and non-Jew. But now it was impossible to say who was on your side and who wasn't; the trust that had prevailed in Jewish Luboml for ages evaporated overnight.

Rumor had it that our teachers of German and Ukrainian were both Nazi spies. Sure enough, when we all posed for the class photo at the end of the school year, those two turned their heads away at the last instant and were not in the picture.

Neighbor informed upon neighbor. A petty personal grudge could result in an accusation of counterrevolutionary activity. Even punishing a child for misbehavior could cause him to retaliate with charges of disloyalty against his elders. A youngster could also cause great harm unwittingly, repeating something said at the dinner table without realizing its meaning. For that reason, most adults made a point of never discussing politics at home.

A saying made the rounds—this sort of gallows humor was commonplace under communism—that the population was divided into three categories: those who are in prison, those who were in prison, and those who will be in prison. And the overcrowded jails were horrific: holding pens for interrogation, torture, and then deportation.

You never knew what could get you into trouble. For example, I had two older cousins, brother and sister, who had fled from the Nazi-occupied zone across the Bug River and were among more than a thousand refugees who flooded our town in the first few months of the war. They stayed in our cramped dwelling for a while, but with no work and no house of their own, their situation was so grim that, like many others, they decided to return home, crazy as that seemed. In June 1940, they formally registered their request with the Soviets—who promptly interpreted it as an act of disloyalty.

The young woman was arrested in the middle of the night and slated for deportation to Siberia, but for some reason her brother remained free. My mother, worried about the safety of her niece, insisted that he go with her, and with much reluctance he finally agreed. She would die of hunger in a desolate labor camp, but he would survive the ordeal. Ironically, Jews who were sent to Siberia turned out to be the lucky ones: they had a much higher survival rate than those of us who would be caught in the Nazi net.

In November 1940, Shneyer was drafted into the Red Army. He was part of a huge call-up of boys born between 1918 and 1920. Hundreds of youths in our town were now torn from their homes.

Anyone familiar with the history of Eastern Europe knows how young Jews tried to starve or injure themselves to avoid serving in the Czar's army—my father was one of them—and this remained the case under Polish rule between the wars. Before their pre-induction physicals, young men in Luboml often went without sleep or proper food for weeks at a time and at night roamed around the city in packs. Shneyer and his friends tried to weaken themselves by fatigue, dehydration, and a bad diet—I can still recall his bleary, red eyes—but it didn't work. The Soviet state would not be so easily fooled.

The recruits left from the train station and my family, like countless others, walked across town to see them off. It was a solemn, silent procession that grew in size until we reached the railway cars where the young men, already in uniform and shorn of their hair, were about to go onboard.

For the first time we found out that Shneyer had a girlfriend, who had also come to say goodbye. But most tightly of all he embraced our mother, with whom he had the strongest bond of any of her three children. Not surprisingly for a young man in full view of his peers, Shneyer kept his emotions in check. But Mameh soon became agitated at the thought of her first born going away. The Soviet Union was not yet a belligerent, but with the war raging in Western Europe, she had a premonition that the pact between Hitler and Stalin would not last. Weeping and then shrieking, she wouldn't let go of him.

I thought her near-hysterical behavior strange and silly. Why the huge fuss? I wondered. My big brother is leaving for two years with a lot of other boys, and then they'll all come home. There must have been a band or patriotic songs at the farewell that day, but all I remember is a loud whistle before the train pulled out of the terminal.

Shneyer was soon posted to an artillery battalion in Kostroma, a town with a frigid climate three hundred miles northeast of Moscow. As the other mothers did for their sons in the service, Mameh sent him food packages. He shipped us silk stockings (where he got them, I have no idea) and fabric that could be made into dresses for my mother and me. Shneyer wrote us frequently about the elaborate military parades, for which the horses' legs were wrapped with decorative white cloth. But his letters, pored over by a military censor, also hinted at the horrors of the Soviet system. He spoke of the preponderance of insane asylums, and much later we would learn that these were the destination of many a dissident.

The Nazi-Soviet war broke out only eight months after Shneyer joined the army, the month after I turned sixteen. Because Luboml was so close to the border, we were bombed in

My brother Shneyer (top row, center) and Red Army comrades, late 1940 or early 1941.

the early morning hours on the first day of hostilities, June 22, 1941. Within 72 hours, we were overrun by the Wehrmacht. The mighty Red Army proved no match for the blitzkrieg.

Standing on a main road, my mother and I saw thousands of ragged Soviet troops, their hands behind their heads, being marched out of town by a dozen German soldiers. The column of the defeated seemed to stretch for miles into the distance. Under the hot sun, the prisoners looked hungry and thirsty, dejected and lifeless. Years later I thought of that scene when I heard the old saw about Jews going to their deaths "like sheep to the slaughter." Here were trained military men who vastly out-numbered their German guards, yet could not have been more submissive.

But at the time Mameh and I thought only about Shneyer, who might be suffering a similar fate. We ran to our house, got pails of water and a few drinking cups, and rushed back to the long, long line of captives. But we never slaked the thirst of a single POW. As soon as we held out our offering, a German guard pushed us back with a rifle butt to our bellies.

3 | My Prison

IN THE OPENING DAYS OF the German invasion of the USSR, even before our town fell, Tateh had come to the conclusion that we had to flee to Russia. He wanted us to go east with his Soviet employees from the sawmill, who were quickly evacuating Luboml en masse and taking their goods and equipment with them. Yet my mother refused to leave. "How will Shneyer find us?" she fretted. Mameh couldn't bear the thought of her son returning from the army to an abandoned home with no way of contacting his family.

But once she saw the Wehrmacht brutalizing Jews on the streets, she gave in. It was now too late for us to join the Soviet convoy, but father had another plan: On our own, we would first make our way to Kovel, a railway hub about fifty kilometers east, and from there catch a Russia-bound train. It meant entering a world of uncertainty, but he was sure a far greater danger awaited us if we remained.

The families of the three brothers and two sisters he had in Luboml stayed put, and indeed very few Volhynian Jews went on the road in June 1941. It was known that German planes strafed columns of refugees, Ukrainian gangs beat and robbed them, and the routed Red Army no longer offered any protection. Those of us fleeing Luboml were at a further disadvantage: Starting out on the western edge of the province, we would have to traverse almost all of war-torn Volhynia just to cross the pre-1939 border between Poland and the USSR. Even if we made it, no one knew for certain that we'd be allowed in.

My father was in a better position than most. Because of his high post in the sawmill, he was easily able to commandeer a horse and wagon for the trip to Kovel. Also, he figured his fluency in Russian and the connections he had made with his Soviet workers during the occupation would serve him later.

We buried our valuables—clothing, bedspreads, dishes, tools—in a sunken bin under a shed adjoining our house. Onto the open cart we piled two featherbeds, a few pillows, winter coats, and some food. My mother took along the two silver candlesticks she had received on her wedding day and some top-quality cloth. My parents and I rode in the wagon with Meir beside us on our family's one bicycle.

It was happening so quickly. Without even a goodbye, I was abandoning my friends, my school, my aunts, uncles, and cousins and venturing into the unknown. In an instant everything I'd thought was so stable had collapsed. But I still had my parents and Meir; they now became my whole life. I didn't want to leave Luboml, where I'd spent all of my sixteen years, but I had complete trust in my father's judgment that we had no other choice.

We set out early and made good time in the mild weather on flat terrain. There were fewer signs of the war than we'd feared. To ease the horse's burden, we walked alongside the wagon for part of the journey but still reached the outskirts of Kovel by nightfall. Then we stopped and waited while Meir biked to the railway station to inquire about the train. He returned in about an hour with the bad news: it was too late. The last train had left the station—Meir had actually glimpsed it in the distance—and now the Germans had closed the rail line at Kovel. We had to head back to Luboml.

At first I was overcome with relief. Now I could go home, I thought, and pick up the threads of my prior life, which I'd feared had been cut forever that very morning.

Suddenly a new worry seized me—what to do with the Komsomol ID card I carried close to my bosom. Returning to German-occupied territory, I could be killed for being a Communist if the Nazis discovered it on me. But if I threw it away and the Soviets ever re-conquered our region, I'd be sent to Siberia if I couldn't produce it. I told my mother of the dilemma and she settled the matter. Rip it up into small pieces, she advised me, and leave it in a public toilet. I did, and felt that was the right place for it all along.

With our horse showing weariness, we took two days for the trip home, staying overnight with some relatives in the village of Macheve. From there to Luboml we endured a harrowing journey. By now thousands of steel-helmeted German infantrymen were pouring across the province. As we rode west, they moved east on the same narrow road—and frequently struck us with rifles, clubs, or whips. We had no choice but to ride directly into that storm of thugs. Beating us and other bedraggled refugees was simply sport for the Wehrhmacht. You could see the glee in their eyes. Tateh and Meir bore the brunt of it; within a few hours blood ran down their faces and arms.

When we finally reached Luboml, the acrid smell of smoke told the story of what had happened during our three-day absence: Much of the town, including the heart of the Jewish section, had been burned to the ground. The Great Synagogue was unscathed, but the residential quarter lay in ruins.

We rushed to Chelmska Street and found almost nothing left of our house but ashes and blackened wood. The roof, the walls, all our furniture had been devoured by the flames. The subterranean bin was still there but our goods were missing. Only one stone step remained of our home, a cruel mockery of everything we'd had. Not only was my childhood gone, but my childhood home as well.

Who had burned Jewish Luboml? Most likely the Germans, although I've also heard the blame put on the Ukrainians, who went on a rampage against the Jews throughout Volhynia at this time.

Where could we go? My father's brother Simcha's large house was still standing, but it was already packed with refugees from the fire. We latecomers had paid a high toll for our failed trip to Kovel. There was no choice but to move in with the family of my mother's sister Tziril, the poor relations from whom I had felt little warmth since I was a small girl.

They lived almost a mile from us, on the eastern edge of the Jewish section. Before the war my parents had tried to help them, providing most of the firewood to heat their home and sending me to deliver milk and cheese. But while I liked the eldest of their four school-aged children, a bright, lively boy named Meir like my brother, I never felt comfortable with his parents. Tziril and her husband, who scratched out a living trading livestock and was idle a lot of the time, took the dairy products from my hands without genuine appreciation. I think Tziril, who was a beautiful woman but had never been out of Luboml, was jealous of my mother: of the good life and nice things Mameh had, and of her years in the cosmopolitan capital.

Now we were forced to live in that house—nothing more than a kitchen, another room, and a tiny attic. There was an unfinished room, too, but with a dirt floor and gaps in the walls and roof, it was deemed uninhabitable. This hovel, painted gray, was located just within the boundaries of the ghetto the Germans would set up later in the year. In total, we stayed there fifteen months until the end. Mameh, who had reigned like a queen on Chelmska Street, was in anguish the whole time at Tziril's; I could read the suffering on her face.

The ten of us were soon joined by two others whom I loved dearly: my mother's widowed sister, Lieberosha, who taught me how to knit, and her handsome son, Yidl. In his mid-twenties, Yidl had walked the 225 kilometers to Luboml from Warsaw, where things were even worse. Still wearing his suit from the big city, he infused some life into the place by telling us kids about the great metropolis on the Vistula; that was the only entertainment we had. Tziril's son Meir, meanwhile, spent a lot of time in the attic engrossed in the study of English because he wanted to immigrate to America after the war. We still marked the arrival of Shabbes—by lighting candles inserted into a potato—but any moment of serenity was fleeting. One of us always had to keep an eye out the window.

Months later another family of four would arrive from Nudyze: my mother's favorite brother, Hershel, his wife, and their adorable little son and daughter. We would then be sixteen people, sharing a living space of less than seven hundred square feet, typical for the Jews of Luboml under Nazi rule.

Early on, my father tried to spare me the suffering he knew lay ahead. He arranged for me to go into hiding in a nearby village with a Ukrainian peasant family who owed him a favor. The man of the house came to Tziril's to meet me; he was younger than Tateh, tall, robust and red-cheeked. Wearing fine leather boots, he seemed relatively prosperous.

Yet I knew nothing about him or his wife and children and was scared about going off with a stranger. Most of all, I had never been apart from my family before and I couldn't imagine leaving them now. Tateh quickly understood and did not try to persuade me. We would remain together.

It wasn't long before we felt the full horror of the occupation. Only days after we moved in, father came home deeply shaken. He was one of about a hundred Jewish men who had been assembled in the main square and ordered to bring brooms, pails, and shovels to clean the streets. They worked for a few hours and were then addressed by the German commandant. He announced that Jewish saboteurs had cut the telephone lines from Luboml to another town—such ridiculous pretexts would frequently be given by the Nazis—and now a price had to be paid.

The Jews were made to count off in consecutive numbers and every twentieth—five in all—were pulled out and marched up to Jagiellonian Hill facing the center of town. There they were summarily executed, the gunfire heard by all. A few Jews were told to go up and retrieve the bodies, which were later buried in the Jewish cemetery. Tateh knew all of those murdered, and one of them, Shmuel Weingarten, a prominent textile merchant, had lived across the street from us on Chelmska Street. How my life had changed! Before the war, I'd envied his son's shiny bicycle.

This opening round was clearly intended to send us a message about obedience, and the Germans imposed severe restrictions from the outset. On penalty of death, Jews were forced to turn over all their money and gold to the authorities, abide by a curfew from 6 p.m. to 6 a.m., and wear a white armband with a blue Star of David. That could easily be slipped on and off, or covered by an outer layer of clothing, but a couple of months later—on Yom Kippur eve—a new decree mandated that we sew two yellow patches on our coats, one on the front and one on the back.

We were not even allowed to use the sidewalks, but had to walk in the street. Filled with shame, I feared my gentile former schoolmates or teachers would point me out and yell "Yid!" or even worse, if they knew of my Komsomol affiliation, "Communist!" Mameh was humiliated in another way. I don't know the reason for the decree, but Jewish women were not permitted to wear hair below their earlobes, and my mother had to cut the long, beautiful braid that she wound over her head. She no longer looked like the same woman.

The men were required to elect a *Judenrat*, a council of twelve to carry out the Nazi regulations and deliver to the occupiers everything from furs and gold to pots and pans. Its chairman was Kalman Kopelzon, a respected pharmacist whom my parents knew well. I know of the controversy surrounding the Judenrat leaders in the big cities like Lodz and Warsaw, who have been accused of favoritism, corruption, and worse. But few of us in my shtetl ever felt that way about Kopelzon, who was himself beaten and ultimately executed in a bloody pit. We thought he did the best he could in an impossible situation. Rumor had it that because of his intervention "only" five were executed on Jagiellonian Hill.

Still, my father declined Kopelzon's request to join the Judenrat. I think Tateh had an idea of what that job would require of him and could not bring himself to play God with the lives of his neighbors.

The Judenrat oversaw the distribution of food, and the rations were so paltry that to supplement our diet we slowly had to barter away the few belongings we had left. We were each entitled to one slice of bread daily, called "10-deko" because it supposedly weighed ten decagrams, or about three and a half ounces. It provided a few hundred calories at most. Made of rye flour, it was dark and moist and tasted like clay. I craved real bread and often dreamed about eating it with another luxury we almost never had, butter.

One of my cousins dispensed the so-called bread in our neighborhood, and sometimes she'd slip me an extra piece, but there was never enough for our hungry household. My mother insisted that she and I give some of our portion to Tateh and Meir, because they went out to do manual labor all day, while we were usually at home. I never questioned her decision. She tried to make the bread go as far as possible, often cooking it in a broth along with whatever she could scrounge: a potato or potato peels, herbs, and even beet leaves. Meat, expressly forbidden for Jewish consumption, was the rarest commodity in the ghetto.

My family had one possession that could be traded for a good deal of food on the street, but mother was loath to give it up—cuts of fine, pinstriped English wool, which she intended to make into two suits for Shneyer upon his return from the army. Still, we subsisted, and in rural Volhynia there were few cases of Jews dying of starvation as they did in the big Polish cities west of us. But I cannot remember a moment in Tziril's house when my stomach was full.

Even worse than the malnutrition was the forced labor to which we were all subjected. Some, like my father and brother, were relatively fortunate in having permanent jobs in the sawmill, which continued to operate under the Nazis. Tateh was demoted from supervisor, and he and Meir labored long hours with little food and were abused by Germans, Ukrainians, and sometimes the Jewish police. Yet at least the work itself was not life-threatening. Those like myself, who lacked the prized certificates proving employment, could be caught like dogs by the authorities and literally worked to death.

To protect me from these dreaded *chappers* (catchers, as we called them in Yiddish), Tateh landed me a job as a maid and field hand on the nearby estate of the Ukrainian head of the sawmill. I wasn't used to this kind of labor—cleaning pigsties and digging potatoes out of the ground—and came home with blistered hands. But I was deeply grateful for the work. Aside from the safety it provided, the lady of the house often served me a real meal and, even better, handed me some carrots and beets to bring home for my family. How proud I felt to be able to add to our meager food supply!

Unfortunately my job on the estate lasted only about a month, and soon thereafter I was grabbed by a German soldier on the street and taken in a van to a train yard on the outskirts of town.

There, with other Jewish teenagers, mostly girls, I was made to perform the most grueling tasks: lugging steel rails back and forth, moving piles of earth in wheelbarrows, and unloading heavy equipment from trucks. The shift lasted ten hours, and any slowdown resulted in a whipping. Two years earlier, when the Soviets had annexed eastern Poland, they had widened the tracks to conform to their own railway system. Now the Germans, eager to supply their advancing armies on the eastern front, made us slave to put the rails back in their original position.

Frail and undernourished, it is not surprising that I collapsed within a few days. Lifting a weighty beam, I wrenched my back and was in terrific pain but had to keep working. Each night I limped home and was awakened at dawn the next morning by a Jewish policeman who escorted me to the workers' assembly point. Finally, it became obvious even to him that I could barely move, and he let me remain in bed. But I had done permanent damage to several disks in my back, causing me pain and discomfort all the years since.

The lumbar injury spared me further work on the railroad, but my plight, and that of my dear parents and brother, sent me into a tailspin of depression. I suffered bouts of fever, severe headaches, and frequent respiratory infections, no doubt worsened by our horrible diet and cramped quarters. Nor did we have enough heating fuel; in the winter, ice formed on the inside windows and walls of Tziril's house.

Now at age sixteen I was still not menstruating. It took courage for me to discuss such an intimate matter with my mother, who took me to Dr. Amshchibovsky. Gravely, he told Mameh there was nothing more he could do and it really didn't matter anyway because none of us would survive the ghetto. I would not have another period until after the war.

About a month into the occupation the green-uniformed SS, with a death's-head insignia on their hats, implemented the first phase of their policy of extermination. On July 22, they seized almost four hundred Jewish men on the streets or in their homes, drove them to a ravine several miles away, and shot them to death in ditches. Thankfully, neither Tateh nor Meir, hiding in an attic above the sawmill, was among them, nor were any of the other males in our household rounded up. About a month later, a second mass murder claimed nearly four hundred more lives, including women, and again we were spared. Amidst all this misery, I realized I was one of the lucky ones.

The *Einsatzgruppen*, the mobile SS units that carried out those massacres in the summer of 1941, left Volhynia after killing about 10 percent of the Jewish population, and moved east on the heels of the advancing German army. The same commandos would decimate scores of other Jewish communities in the Ukraine.

After the SS left Luboml, the ferocity continued under German military rule. The *Gebietskommissar*, or district commander,

a tall, blonde officer in his late thirties named Uhde, was mon-
strous in his cruelty. In mid-1942, he personally executed three
teenaged girls (two sisters and their cousin) for smuggling—they
had traded kerchiefs to a Ukrainian peasant for bread, milk, and
eggs—but first he extorted a high ransom from the Judenrat,
which had hoped to buy their freedom. A shocked Kopelzon
witnessed the shootings. Then Uhde told him and the other Jewish leaders present that the Germans had kept their part of the
bargain by "turning over the prisoners." By that he meant that
Kopelzon and a family member of the slain girls were allowed
to remove the corpses. This story spread quickly through the
ghetto (and was later confirmed by several survivors, including
one eyewitness who testified at Uhde's trial in West Germany in
1961). At the time I heard something else, that was probably just
a rumor but has been repeated by Luboml survivors to this day:
One of the young girls was so petrified that just before the executions her hair turned gray.

For the amusement of his soldiers, Uhde caught religious men
on the streets, beat them, sliced off their beards, and then made
them urinate on Torah scrolls. When German troops accidentally
came across an age-old Purim *megillah* in the Great Synagogue,
he ordered it burned. Most horrifying to me was that he let one
of his underlings, another Wehrmacht officer, with a big dog,
come into the Jewish quarter and simply shoot people for the
fun of it. For some reason this target practice was always on a
Wednesday, and that day of the week, on which other tragedies
would occur later, still causes me dread.

Through it all, the bestial Commandant Uhde had time for a
love affair. He spent most nights in the boudoir of a young aris-
tocrat, Topka Kampyoni, whom we all referred to as a princess.
Her family owned a vast estate of orchards, livestock, and rich
farmland outside Luboml.

Before the war, the attractive, long-limbed Topka, a noted equestrienne, was frequently spotted on the back roads in her elegant riding attire. She and her noble family had had to flee during the Soviet occupation, of course, but after the German invasion the Kampyonis returned and took back all their holdings. We knew of Topka's relationship with Uhde because Jewish men, including Tateh, Meir, and Uncle Hershel, were often forced to uproot weeds and trees on her estate on Sundays, and they frequently saw the two together. Also, a Jewish teenager whom we knew, Avrum Getman, who worked for the Kampyonis and lived in Topka's large country house, confirmed the intimate arrangement they had. After the war, when the Soviets again seized her lands, she married Uhde and moved to Germany with him.

Kopelzon may have hoped that Topka would be a moderating influence on Uhde, or at least a source of inside information, but if so he was badly mistaken. The Gebietskommissar never showed us a bit of mercy, and the extent of his savagery always seemed to take the Judenrat by surprise. Topka provided us no help and simply exploited free Jewish labor.

Many other Ukrainians treated us a lot worse. The Nazis, vicious as they were, would not have been able to confine, enslave, and ultimately annihilate the Jews of Eastern Europe had it not been for the willing help of the locals. In our region the Ukrainians were enthusiastic henchmen. Taking advantage of our helplessness, they robbed, raped, and killed us with abandon. At the beginning of the occupation the Germans empowered them to form a police force, and it dealt with us ruthlessly, even rounding up Jews for the mass executions carried out by the SS.

With the aid of the Ukrainian police, the ghetto was formed in early December 1941, further tightening the noose around our necks. Unlike larger cities, Luboml's ghetto was not completely sealed, but fences and barbed wire were erected in many places. We could see the barrier through the back window of Tziril's house. Now food was now even harder to obtain because our ability to barter with non-Jewish peasants and townsfolk was curtailed. But my father, putting his life on the line, occasionally traded for edibles over the fence in Tziril's yard, which separated us from a flourmill on the other side of the ghetto. One time he exchanged some sewing materials for real bread.

Many Jews from the outlying villages were transferred into the ghetto, and Uncle Hershel and his family came from Nudyze to join us. We were tightly confined: Except for work, going outside the area of a few hundred square yards was punishable by death.

Other decrees followed, including a ban on all Jewish learning. But at Tziril's house we managed to conduct some text study for boys. My great-uncle Rabbi Moishe Shneyers Povroshnik, a beloved, black-coated *melamed*, came over several times a week to teach Bible and some Talmud to my young cousins and a couple of other kids from down the street.

One time, with the men of the house away at work, a German officer walked by and heard the children repeating some Hebrew words. We always kept the front door locked, but he burst through the side door of the unfinished room and was soon upon us. With his riding crop he whipped the elderly Moishe Shneyers across the face until blood dripped onto the holy books. Then he turned on his heel and left the way he came in, through the partially completed room of the house. In anger he kicked a mound of dirt and uncovered my mother's two cherished candlesticks. Then he came back and hit all of us with his whip, even the small children.

He didn't carry away the ornamental candlesticks—probably he didn't want to risk being seen in the streets with Jewish ceremonial objects in his hands—but he screamed at us that if we didn't turn them into the commandant's office we'd be shot. Mameh and Tateh were too frightened to do otherwise, but Moishe Shneyers showed some defiance. Even after that ghastly episode he returned to teach the youngsters.

A few privileged Jews were permitted to reside outside the ghetto, among them Dr. Amshchibovsky and his brother-in-law, a dentist. At one point they and their family members obtained forged Aryan passports and fled. The Germans and the Judenrat were in an uproar over the escape, and a search party, including some Jews, was sent looking for them, but they were never found. We all knew they would have been hanged in public had they been caught, but we were also afraid that if they remained at large, other Jews would be executed in their stead. This time Uhde was sated merely by levying a big fine on the Jewish community.

My parents were allowed to leave the ghetto for a day, but it was for the worst reason imaginable. In early 1942, word came to us that two Ukrainians had information about my brother Shneyer's status. Along with him, they had been drafted into the Red Army more than a year and a half earlier, and now they had returned to their native village. Filled with foreboding, Mameh and Tateh went to Kopelzon and with his help they obtained safe passage. No doubt he figured that with Meir and me left behind in the ghetto, my folks would not even think of escape.

When they returned at dusk, I knew instantly my brother was dead. Mother wouldn't speak and remained silent for many days thereafter. Through his tears, father told us that Shneyer's two comrades were so bone-thin and weak they had to be propped up on soft cushions. They had been released from a horrendous German POW camp but said that Shneyer didn't make it; he had died there. We never received more details, and to this day I am perplexed about the actual fate of my kindhearted big brother.

My soul was ripped apart but most painful of all was to witness my mother's despair. After she heard the devastating news she did agree to part with the wool meant for Shneyer's suits. It would be traded for several kilos of cereal. But not right away. For a few more weeks she kept the fabric, the last connection to her son, close by.

We were all in agony now, which is the only explanation I have for Aunt Tziril's behavior. She had sustained a great loss, too: her husband, Nuchem, had been caught on the street by the German chappers and forced to lead a team of horses to the Russian front, we were told. We had heard nothing of him for many months and assumed he'd been taken out and shot like so many others captured for "work." Still, none of us was prepared for a venomous remark that Tziril made. In a jeering, taunting way she said to mother: "So, you don't have your *zindeleh*, your darling son, anymore." Mameh almost collapsed after hearing that, and I didn't have the courage to ask her why Tziril had said it. Fortunately, my father was not in earshot, and I would never tell him of those hurtful words.

With knowledge of Shneyer's death, Meir became even more precious to Mameh, Tateh, and me. But like the rest of us, Meir was a changed person in the ghetto. Long gone was the fun-loving, carefree kid who amused and sometimes infuriated us with his antics. By mid-1942 he had been beaten several times, once by a Jewish policeman who slugged him during a work detail on Topka's estate after Meir stepped in to save Uncle Hershel from a thrashing. During the week my brother would return from the long, hard days at the sawmill more than a mile away, fall onto the bed he shared with Tateh, and, without a word or a smile, turn his face to the wall and remain in that position through the night.

Meir could have made things easier for himself and for the rest of us under the Germans. He had been asked to join the Jewish police, which would have meant an extra full loaf of bread for our family every day, a godsend. But just as my father turned down a seat on the Judenrat, my brother passed up this offer too. We all respected Meir's choice. While most of us understood the difficulties faced by the Judenrat officials, we could not condone the brutish behavior of some of the cops who, armed with rubber clubs, bloodied their fellow Jews. This was bad enough in the big cities, but appalling in a shtetl like Luboml where everybody knew everybody else.

Meir would take an altogether different path. In the late summer of 1942 he began to meet regularly with a group of youths a few blocks away. Sometimes my mother sent me there to fetch him. I gleaned they were planning to escape, though none of the details were spoken in my presence.

By then there was no limit to our desperation. The clear-thinking ones among us began to realize that a new phase of killings was taking place across Volhynia—not massacres of a portion of the Jewish population, but rather the liquidation of entire communities.

Kopelzon's daughter and son-in-law were perhaps the first to tell such a tale, no doubt against the wishes of the Judenrat chairman. They arrived from Rovno early in 1942 and spread the incredible news that the SS had exterminated almost all of that city's 25,000 Jews. In August, our own relatives came to Luboml from Kamen-Kashirski with a similar story about their small town, made "clean" of the Jews, *judenrein*, in the parlance of the killers. The next month, one of my cousins and her two daughters literally ran to us from her village twenty-five kilometers away. "There are no more Jews in Macheve," she gasped, and while the information was hard to fit into our brains, we knew deep down it was just a matter of time before we too would be hit. The prospect of Luboml being the next target was spoken in a whisper; adults didn't want children to hear it.

The most ominous development had actually occurred a couple of months earlier: the deployment of dozens of Jews as forced laborers to dig four long, deep ditches at a brick-making factory in the nearby hamlet of Borki. The Germans gave all sorts of benign reasons for the job, such as excavating clay for the manufacture of pots, but it was hard to escape the feeling that the men were digging graves—their own and those of their townsmen.

On one of the last evenings of September 1942, my brother took Mameh, Tateh, and me aside. Holding a knapsack with some clothes and a stash of dried-out bread he had hoarded under a floorboard, Meir said the time had come for him to leave for the woods with his friends. (They numbered about thirty, and later I learned they had one gun among them.) My parents fully approved, of course. They longed for him to survive, and this was his best chance.

My only thought was to go with him. I would have done anything to get out of that doomed place. But he refused. Mameh pleaded with him to take me, and she cried uncontrollably, but he wouldn't budge. The group would not allow girls or anyone under eighteen, Meir said, and he thought of me as a very young seventeen. He was well aware of my poor health, too, and of course I had not been involved in any of the preparations for the mission.

As he departed, Meir must have believed I'd soon be murdered along with our parents.

Yet I've never blamed him for leaving me behind. He had to think first of the welfare of his comrades with whom he had carefully planned the flight to freedom. For a kid sister to show up at the last minute was against their rules and not realistic. If anything, I pity him for the way he had to leave us; he must have been in torment. Such heartrending farewells took place in a thousand Jewish households across Volhynia that summer and early fall as young people left their families for the forest.

The obliteration of the Jews of Luboml began a couple of days later. Just before dawn on October 1, the holiday of Hashanah Rabbah, we heard dozens of trucks enter the town and knew it was the SS. At first light we glimpsed the Ukrainian police walking in formation behind them.

It was time to enter our hiding place. For weeks my resourceful father had been preparing a refuge for us, and we had gone in several times on trial runs.

He used heaps of lumber in the unfinished room of Tziril's home: long, flat boards that none of the rest of us ever touched because they were intended to complete the house. Over a period of weeks Tateh piled them one on top of the other, almost to the roof, about fifteen feet in length and three feet from a windowless wall, which abutted a small stable. He fashioned a tiny door at one end of the hiding place, made of the same boards, which he could close from the inside by pulling a little handle made of rope. To any intruder it would look like one huge woodpile stacked neatly against the wall.

Since Luboml was one of the very last Volhynian towns to be liquidated, many households had time to set up such hideaways, or *shronen*—in cellars, sheds, tunnels, or anyplace that might conceal them. But there were also plenty of ghetto-dwellers who were unprepared when the day of reckoning arrived. They had to depend on the kindness of their neighbors to shelter them from the murderers.

Our house was no longer as crowded as it had been. Tziril's husband was long gone, and Uncle Hershel's family of four, able to obtain a room nearby, had moved out shortly before the end. My brother, of course, had just set out, and two of the other young men among us, my cousins Meir and Yidl, ran off at the first sign of the SS. Their goal was not to fight back from the forest but rather to reach an outlying village and go into hiding.

Other Jews took the places of those who had left. The newcomers were nearby residents who had somehow learned of our hiding place, and came seeking refuge. My father refused no one but was highly ambivalent. He was especially concerned about our next-door neighbor, the widowed teacher Bluma Mezch, a relative of Tziril's husband. She brought along her elderly father-in-law and her two children, aged one and three. As that family entered our house, the rest of us felt a heightened sense of dread. We didn't even have to speak our fears of one of those tots crying at the wrong time.

When we saw two big, heavy pillows in Bluma's hands, we realized the brutal bargain she had struck with my father.

Bluma, her children, and the older Mezch went in first; they would be the deepest into the hiding place. Five other neighbors followed, as did Tziril and three of her kids, my Aunt Lieberosha, and then my mother and I. Tateh, the last in, shut the door behind himself. In all, there were sixteen of us.

We sat silently on the earthen floor, our knees close to our chests, in two rows facing one another. A bit of light came in from spaces between the rough-hewn boards and from the narrow gap between the lumber pile and the roof. My father had brought in a pail of water but was unable to stockpile any food. And of course we had no way to go to the toilet. Cramped though we were, he probably could have brought in a bucket for human waste, but he preferred us not moving up and down that makeshift narrow corridor; he wanted us to stay in place. Also, even in this life-or-death situation, considerations of modesty may have been a factor. The thought of women lifting their skirts and squatting over a pail might have been more than he could abide.

Clearly, Tateh was counting on a short stay in the hiding place, four or five hours at most. This was a reasonable assumption given the roundups and executions that had occurred in Luboml the previous summer and the liquidations of entire Volhynian towns over the past few months. SS men and Ukrainian police typically swept through a community for half a day and then left the area.

Luboml turned out differently. As nowhere else in the province, the "Jew-hunt" went on for almost a full week.

On the first day about 1,800 Jews were rounded up and machine-gunned in the freshly dug ditches of the brick factory in Borki. Thousands more were killed after that at other execution sites, on the streets, or in their homes. Because many Jews had been transferred from the villages to our town during 1942, the Jewish population neared 8,000 by the time the carnage began. Fewer than a thousand survived the October massacres, and only 51 would live to see the end of the war.

As the first day of the liquidation wore on, we could hear the pandemonium outside—gunfire and motors, shouts and wails. It never seemed to let up. To leave the hiding place would be suicidal.

Yet the pressure of staying became greater with every passing hour. Our water supply gave out fast, most of it going to the demanding children. Aunt Lieberosha, bless her soul, had a tiny linen sack in which she kept a tomato. She moistened our lips with it, but that wasn't enough to quench our growing thirst.

Bluma's father-in-law was the first to lose his mind under this stress. In the early afternoon he suddenly stood up and insisted on chanting prayers for Hashanah Rabbah. It was a Jewish holiday, he loudly declared, and he was going to *daven*. Tateh quickly stepped over several of us and reached him. He put his hand over the old man's mouth and dragged him out of the hiding place. Then, at great risk, father carried him through the unfinished room into the main part of the house, deposited him on one of the beds, and hurried back to our refuge.

We heard him praying but not for long. Someone entered the house, shot him dead, and left. We all shuddered but were hardly shocked. By then death had become all too familiar.

Other break-ins followed. There was only one brief visit of heavy-booted German speakers, thankfully without a dog, and they poked around with their bayonets before leaving. But every few hours we'd hear the voices of Ukrainian police or peasants. They looted the few belongings we still had and looked around the unfinished room as well. In time they probably would have begun to haul off the wood that concealed us, but for now they were searching for valuables—and for Jews.

Each time we sensed an invader, we barely breathed. Bluma pushed a pillow down on the face on each of her babies; thank God neither was suffocated. We remained undetected and made it through the night.

By the second day the hopelessness of our situation was obvious. While the killing raged outside, we realized that the hiding place could be a death chamber too. Our thirst had now become unbearable; it was hard to think of anything else. We were ravenously hungry as well, but somehow that wasn't as bad. You could doze off even while famished. But the dryness on our lips and tongues, in our mouths and throats, was pure torture.

Tateh remembered that a tall jar of *kvass,* or bread soup, had been left in the kitchen and, taking his life in his hands again, ran out and brought it back. We passed it around and drank greedily, but the sour, salty liquid only added to our thirst. The lack of water, I thought, will drive us mad. My mother, a tower of strength from my earliest memory, was beginning to mutter nonsense to herself, and her delirium scared me no end.

I became terrified about something else as well. With no other options, we'd had to relieve ourselves right where we were sitting. By the second day the stink generated by fifteen people was awful, and I was sure some Ukrainian prowler would suspect it came from human beings and not from the adjoining stable.

After nightfall, when the commotion on the ghetto streets quieted down, I gave my father advice for the first time in my life: "The stench will give us away," I whispered, "We have to get out of here now, whatever the danger." He nodded.

4 | Fugitives in the Forest

Bluma Mezch stayed in the hiding place, holding her two small children close to her breast. I will never know if they starved to death there or if they were caught and executed. Also remaining were some of our neighbors, broken in body and soul by the forty-eight-hour confinement and fearful of facing the killing machine outside. My family—half-insane with thirst and aching in our bones—emerged from that hellhole in the middle of the second night.

My parents and I, Aunt Liberosha, and Aunt Tziril and her three kids headed for the woods. To avoid being seen, even at night, we crawled on all fours, first through a break in the ghetto fence not far from Tziril's backyard and then across grassy fields. I crept just behind my mother and father. Mameh, revived by the fresh air, was fast becoming her former self.

Soon the midnight quiet was pierced by a burst of gunfire. Lieberosha, who had poor eyesight and couldn't keep up with us, had gone off in another direction and was shot by a Ukrainian policeman. In the dark, we could only suspect what had happened. But later someone confirmed it: He told us of coming across the body of a woman clutching a little sack that contained a tomato.

After a few hundred meters on our hands and knees, we finally reached the last street. Beyond it lay pastureland and ultimately the refuge of the forest. But we knew that Luboml was ringed with Ukrainian guards who had orders to shoot escaping Jews on sight.

Tateh had a plan and told the six of us to crouch down beside the wall of a nearby house. Then he approached a Ukrainian guard and handed him a stack of phony American dollars. Allowed to cross the road alone, he disappeared into the black night. An instant later a shot rang out. Had he just been killed? My mother quickly left me with Tziril's family and darted between sentries in search of her husband. If he lay wounded, maybe she could help him.

Another volley of bullets from across the street, the same direction where Mameh had run. Now I was certain that both my parents had just been murdered. My entire world collapsed. I was frozen, not by fear, but by something greater: With Mameh and Tateh gone, nothing in the whole universe mattered anymore.

I stared blankly at Tziril. She neither consoled nor comforted me. She simply said, "Come on, let's go," and motioned me to follow her and her children, not to the woods but in another direction.

I neither answered nor moved. I had no room in my mind for any thought beyond my parents being dead. Going anyplace at that moment, or doing anything, would be utterly without purpose.

Aunt Tziril didn't ask twice. She and her kids moved on,

and I lay crumpled on the ground. A short while ago there had been seven of us there. Now I was the only one left. I fully expected a Ukrainian thug to finish me off at any moment, and I didn't care.

Instead, out of the blackness, my mother's face appeared. Was this her ghost? "Mameh, how can you be here? You're dead," I gasped.

"I'm alright, and Tateh is alright," she said, stroking my hair, taking my hand, and leading me to the street.

But we still had to surmount one more hurdle. A Ukrainian cop held Mameh and me at gunpoint even though my father had just bribed him to let us through. Mother pleaded with the youth, an acquaintance of Shneyer's, but we were allowed to pass only when she pressed her wedding ring into his hand. It had been hidden in Tziril's house during the entire German occupation, but before we entered the hiding place Mameh retrieved it and put it on her finger. That ring saved our lives.

Once we found Tateh on the other side of the road, we began to run toward mother's village of Nudyze. Having had almost nothing to eat or drink for forty-eight hours, we craved some moisture on our lips, and shortly before dawn we reached a well in front of a farmhouse. As my father started to raise the bucket on a pulley, dogs barked loudly and came toward us. We had to back off. At last we came upon a pond filled with a green slime. Without hesitating, Tateh took off his hat and used it to scoop up the cloudy liquid, which we swallowed gratefully.

By late morning we reached the farmhouse of a man father had befriended before the war, a former Communist who no doubt feared for his own safety and that of his family. When he saw we were close to breaking down from hunger, he offered us real bread such as I had tasted only once in the past year. But along with the food he gave us some horrible news: My cousins

Yidl and Meir, whom we knew had fled the morning the SS entered Luboml, were dead. They'd been murdered just hours earlier by a nearby peasant who coveted Yidl's fine Warsaw suit. We had actually heard the gunshots ourselves, but we had not known their targets.

The murderer had already bragged to his neighbor how he had killed two Jews by luring the ravenous runaways into his barn with the promise of food. "Wait here, and I'll have my wife bake some pirogi for you," he said. Then he returned with the police, who gunned them down. We were later told that he wore Yidl's suit to church the next Sunday.

Tateh's friend harbored us for the rest of the day. We washed ourselves and slept for a while in his barn. But, unwilling to take any further risk—it was widely known that those caught shielding Jews were hanged along with their families—he insisted we leave by nightfall.

Menaced by hostile shepherds and wild dogs, we continued through thicker and thicker woods until we reached Mameh's village. Our only hope was to reunite with my mother's favorite brother, Hershel. A former scout in the Polish Army, he lived in Nudyze and knew its environs as well as anyone did. It may be that my parents and uncle had made plans beforehand to meet there if Luboml was liquidated. But we were afraid to go directly to his home. Hershel and his family had been deported to the ghetto a few months before, and we figured that by now unfriendly Ukrainians were probably occupying the house. So just before we entered Nudyze we stopped in the yard of another peasant my father knew. Like the one the day before, he gave us food, including delicious buttermilk, but he told Wolko—as he called Tateh—that we had to leave right away. "They'll kill me and my family if they find you here," he said.

Tateh had run out of options. Desperate to find his brother-in-law, he implored the man to search for Hershel and bring him to us. Failing that, we'll remain on your property, father said, until you kill us or have us arrested.

We sat there almost the whole day. Our reluctant host went out several times as we nervously awaited our fate. Would he return with Hershel or with the police? Again and again he came back alone. Finally at dusk we spotted him in the distance walking with another person. It was my uncle.

We were elated to see him but then crushed by the story he told: It began four days earlier when the Germans and Ukrainians had swept through Luboml hunting for Jews. Hershel's family temporarily occupied a room only a few houses away from us, but his tall, attractive wife and three-year-old girl were no longer staying with him. My loveable little cousin, so pretty with her rosy cheeks and dark curls, had taken sick with typhus a few weeks before, and she and her mother moved into a makeshift clinic run by the *Judenrat* on the edge of town.

Hershel remained with the couple's other child, a mischievous boy about five, in the house shared with many others. The ground floor was used as a little woolen mill, crowded with looms, spinning wheels, and other machinery. Not surprisingly, the building contained a hiding place: a dank cellar. When the roundup began, the residents and some neighbors lowered themselves one by one into the subterranean chamber through a narrow trapdoor. Hershel stood holding his son's hand, watching the scene behind a maze of conveyor belts. He and his boy were to be the last ones in.

Suddenly there was trouble. A heavy-set woman got stuck in the tight opening to the cellar, and precious minutes went by. Sensing the killers were near, Hershel held back, hoping the lady could be pushed or pulled through the hole by others. He and his son were well concealed behind the machines, but just as an armed SS-man burst into the room, the boy panicked, jerked his hand free, and ran toward the trapped woman. The German easily caught the kid, dragged him out the front door, and threw him into a waiting truck. All the while the boy shouted "Tateh, help me! Tateh, help me!" Yet there was nothing Hershel could do. In pure shock, his only thought was that his wife and daughter might still be alive and that he needed to save his own life in order to help them.

He soon witnessed Ukrainian police rounding up those who had not yet entered the hiding place, brutally tearing the terrified woman out of the trapdoor and then lifting out one doomed person after another. Amidst the commotion Hershel remained undetected. The Jew-hunters probably thought that the boy's "Tateh" was in the cellar or had already been captured.

That night Hershel stealthily made his way to the clinic. He found his wife and daughter's beds empty. They, along with the others in the infirmary, had been among the first victims of the annihilation. Hershel then made his way to Nudyze, dodging Ukrainian gunmen. He arrived two days before we did and went into hiding with a peasant family until word reached him that we were on the outskirts of the village.

Hershel has to be counted among the survivors of the *Aktion* of October 1942. Nonetheless, my parents and I encountered a man destroyed—ripped to pieces by rage, loss, and guilt that even we could not fully imagine. Again and again he repeated to us the last cries of his little boy, "Tateh, help me!" Those words were seared into his brain as if with a branding iron.

We followed him out of Nudyze and into the surrounding forest, where he was familiar with every trail, creek, and bog. Our lives depended on this man: tall and lean, smart and sure, yet traumatized beyond all limits. Every morning, even when it got very cold, he would awake in a sweat after a fitful night. He was prone to fits of coughing as well. I don't know if it was because he was a heavy smoker, or if that, too, was a physical reaction to all he had just been through.

I think we three were all he had left to live for; otherwise he might have committed suicide. He also could have remained in hiding *alone* for the duration of the war—he enjoyed close friendships with numerous peasants throughout the area— but he knew no one who would even consider sheltering four fugitives.

So he tried to keep us alive in the wilderness. The freezing weather would soon be upon us, and we had no illusions about the force of winter in our region. Before the war we'd donned bulky, cotton-lined vests even in our heated home and eaten fruit preserves, honeyed butter, and lots of *shmaltz*, or chicken fat. Now we would be out in the open.

Fortunately, we had each fled Tziril's house in warm clothing that the looters had somehow missed while we were in hiding: My father wore his sheepskin coat, which had a fur collar, and mother put on Tateh's long cloth Shabbes coat, which had a fur lining and neckpiece. Ironically, I went into the forest with the coat mother had made me two years earlier for the *gimnazjum*. It, too, had a fur collar—it would serve me well during an education of a different kind. Of course, every strand of animal hair would draw lice, and they tormented us no end, but without those garments we could not have made it.

Food was a more immediate problem. We carried some bread with us and there were berries and mushrooms to be picked along the way, but I had no idea how we'd sustain ourselves beyond the next day. Nothing was spoken of this, however, and I doubt Hershel had a firm plan.

If my parents and uncle were counting on a miracle, one appeared, a few days after we left Nudyze, in the form of Tichon, a round-faced, Ukrainian peasant in his late thirties.

The first thing I noticed was his feet. We were sitting on the ground in a meadow, resting against some logs, and were startled when he came near. I glanced up and saw a man wearing neither shoes nor boots, but rather the traditional woodsman's footgear—cloth covered with strips of leather and bark wound around his legs and tied by cords from knee to toe. He wore a fur hat and plain felt coat with a rope around the waist. A hatchet dangled from his shoulder. Whether friend or foe, we now had to deal with him.

He looked at me with pity. "You older folks at least have had a chance to live," he said, "but why does that young girl have to suffer? What sin did she commit?" We soon found out that he had a daughter about my age, one of three children, and maybe I reminded him of her, safe and snug at home. Whatever his motivation, he would never cease caring for us. Aside from my family, there is no person to whom I owe so much.

He advised us to move to a spot deeper into the forest and promised to watch over us and bring us provisions. But could we trust him? My father and uncle had heard of Tichon and said he had a shady reputation and a prison record. Still, we decided to do as he said and go further into the woods, but Hershel insisted that to play it safe, we make camp about a hundred meters from Tichon's designated site. My uncle wanted us to have a head start if we needed to run for our lives.

The next day, not knowing whether to expect deliverance or disaster, we saw Tichon and his wife walking toward us, each carrying a pail. They had brought lots of *pirogi* filled with beans, and even a small bottle of vodka. "There will be more of this," Tichon said with a smile.

He also told us we'd be welcome to the potatoes he stored under a layer of straw in an underground bin next to his home, an isolated cottage a couple of kilometers away. But we could come only at certain times. Tichon made a living as a distiller of homemade *samagon*, strong vodka for which the local police were his best customers, even though the moonshine was technically illegal. They visited him all the time, so he devised an ingeniously simple signal for us to know when to approach his property. Next to his front door a long broom leaned against the wall. If the handle was up, it meant all clear; if the brush was up, we had to stay away.

Under the wing of this protector and benefactor, who knew firsthand what it was to be an outcast, we felt there was at least a chance of survival in the forest. But while Tichon provided us food, and much more, we were on our own regarding shelter.

Uncle Hershel knew how to construct a low hut of branches, twigs, leaves, moss, and bark, with a small, pitched roof to shed the rainwater. Father helped him. It was so tiny that the four of us could sleep only on our sides; to lie on your back or stomach was impossible. Hershel wore sheepskin, like my father, and we piled all four coats on top of us. If one person turned at night, the other three would be disturbed. When we were all inside, there wasn't even enough room for food; we hung whatever we had on trees so animals wouldn't scurry off with it.

Whenever unfriendly peasants or shepherds came near, or when Tichon warned us that a cop had heard about us, we had to move right away. About every two weeks on average we built a new hut, though we stayed within a radius of six or seven kilometers in order not to be too far from our guardian angel. Before the freezing weather set in, we tried to make camp on a bit of high ground surrounded by some water. We hoped this might slow down any raiders, but of course we never felt an ounce of security; we lived in constant fear of detection.

Almost as much as we dreaded our enemies, we feared the

elements. We shivered in those flimsy huts until the springtime, six long months away, and spent the entire winter of 1942–43, one of the coldest of the century, almost completely exposed.

Of those like us, who survived the liquidation of the Volhynian ghettos in the summer and early fall by escaping into the woods, many were caught right away and shot by Ukrainian peasants or police. Some were fortunate enough to form Jewish resistance groups or quickly find the Soviet partisans—bands of former Red Army soldiers and local anti-fascists—and join them as fighters or noncombatants. A smaller number were hidden in the homes or barns of friendly farmers. Even fewer endured the winter like we did, with a selfless supporter, to be sure, but without a proper roof over our heads. "Camping out" in the woods past October was not even considered a real option by most fugitives; it was thought of as a death sentence.

Tateh sought to find an indoor refuge at least for me, and even though we had no valuables or money to put up, he thought I might be hidden by a forester he knew. He asked Tichon, who could work wonders, to find him. Sure enough, the woodsman, carrying a shotgun, rode out to our hut. But before I had to make the agonizing choice of whether or not to leave my family, something I'd refused to do in the ghetto when I'd had the chance, the possibility evaporated. The forester was already hiding others and could not accommodate another person. My fate would continue to be linked with that of my parents and uncle.

I often wonder how we made it, surrounded by snowdrifts and enduring temperatures that remained below zero for days on end. Tichon brought us bundles of straw, which we used to seal the hut's entrance and spread over the frozen ground. His wife, Fedora, even wove me a pair of large, luxurious straw slippers.

But none of this could spare us the agony of that winter. True, we could build a fire to cook our food and warm our bodies, but only in the twilight hours when it would be hard for any predator to observe the glow or the smoke and learn our position. And at times Tichon warned us that even at sunset a fire could give us away.

I sat as close to the flames as I could and still I felt numb. Indeed, I singed my legs without knowing it; the burn marks remained on my skin for many years afterward. Anything I wasn't wearing—my shoes, my undershirt—froze during the night. To thaw a piece of clothing with my hands in the morning and then put it on in the frigid air was awful. My fingers, my back, my face, and especially my feet hurt from the cold every day for many months.

We fared a little better with warm food in our stomachs. When it was safe to light a small fire, my uncle took out a little metal pot, packed it tightly with potatoes, sealed it with leaves and moss, and turned it upside down over the heat. I loved the savory potatoes in their crisp skins, but because of the risk of kindling a fire we couldn't count on such a "meal" on a regular basis.

Almost every Sunday Tichon and his wife, often accompanied by their teenaged daughter, repeated their original act of kindness and brought us a big supply of pirogi, vodka, and, on special occasions, bread. My mother, using anything edible she could find in the woods, was sometimes able to prepare potato soup in the metal pot. She served one batch to my father and uncle in a clay tureen (among the handful of utensils Hershel had somehow gotten from the local peasants), and then poured a second serving into that dish for the two of us. Often Mameh lifted a nearly empty wooden spoon to her mouth so that more of the hot, nourishing broth would remain for me.

Even when the forest yielded nothing more than ice, we had one source of food other than Tichon. Hershel knew of a village in the area that produced wool, and one night he sneaked out and brought back yarn and knitting needles. My mother and I now had some work to pass the time; when there was enough daylight we knit sweaters, which Hershel would bring back to the village and exchange for a loaf of bread or a piece of pork.

We tried to make the bread last for a week or more, but, as much as we needed the protein and fat, none of us ever ate the pig flesh. We gave the pork to Tichon, gladly. That refusal to eat *treyf* —and we would have turned down any non-kosher meat—was the only connection to Judaism we still had.

It was an automatic response, and we never deliberated about it. Nor do I recall any deep discussion about the meaning of what had happened to us. Mostly we just sat in the hut, not speaking very much, partly because we knew that our voices would carry far in the frosty air, partly due to the despondency we felt. The closest I came to any entertainment was killing the lice, which plagued us even in the bitterest cold. I had one undershirt and no matter how often I scrubbed it with snow and hung it on a tree to dry, the insects and their eggs returned.

I felt little vengeance at that time, but I longed to inform the world of how we'd been forced to fight for survival. I fantasized that after the war I'd bring the reporters from the greatest newspapers to the forest and show them the very places where we camped.

Amidst all the pain and discomfort I was more conscious than ever of nature's beauty and efficiency. I was fascinated by the little animals that burrowed in the hard ground and somehow knew exactly where to find a long-buried nut. I was awed by the majesty of winter, even though it threatened to take our lives.

We did have an occasional visitor. Tichon encountered other Jews passing through the forest, usually young people traveling alone or in pairs, and he would send them to us mostly to exchange information. We had precious little food to share with a wayfarer, and of course anyone staying the night had to sleep outside our hut.

In one case a "guest" almost brought us to ruin. The young Avrum Lubochiner arrived after being forced to abandon his hiding place in a barn a few kilometers away. His parents had traded all of their worldly possessions to have him sheltered there, and he had been safe for several months. One night, through the walls, he overheard the farmer and some others plotting to kill him. As soon as they walked off he tried to flee but found the barn doors locked. In desperation, he tore off a piece of the thatched roof, climbed down, and ran for his life. He wound up begging for bread at Tichon's, who fed him and sent him to us.

Now Avrum wanted my father and uncle to participate in a plan to get even with his former host. The farmer stored all sorts of food and clothing in the barn, Avrum told us, and we could gain access by digging up the soil underneath. Then we'd make off with a trove of valuable goods to use or barter.

By coincidence, two distant cousins of ours who were hiding in the next village, the brothers Moshe and Mordche Meiterman, were told our current "address" by Tichon and came by our hut while Lubochiner was there. They heard his plan and eagerly agreed to join him. The three of them persuaded Tateh and Hershel, against their better judgment, to go along on the caper. The men in my family worried that news of a major robbery might stir up the local peasants, most of whom already thought of Jewish refugees as bandits. But the desperate desire to improve our wretched living conditions overcame all objections.

The five men departed the hut at night, leaving Mameh and me trembling from fright as well as from the cold. When the pale winter sun rose and they still hadn't returned, we were close to panic. As we later found out, it took them much longer than expected to tunnel under the barn, and at daybreak the robbers had to race home, losing many of their stolen items along the way. Furthermore, the haul was almost worthless—boxes of rags, cloth, and light summer apparel that we eventually gave away. Worst of all was the fresh trail, from the scene of the crime to our hut, marked not only by footprints, but also by dropped and discarded articles at every turn. We had no choice but to pack up immediately and seek another spot in the forest. Mameh, who had naturally been relieved once the men returned safely, soon bewailed the reckless venture. "All of this for *shmattehs!*" she cried. The Meitermans soon went their own way, as did Lubochiner. It wasn't hard to divide the booty among us.

By early March we had survived the worst of the winter, but Tichon gravely told us we needed to move on. The area had become infested with bands of Ukrainian nationalists, he warned. They had just killed some Jews betrayed by a fire they'd lit at the wrong time, and now they were tracking us. These were the Bulbutzye, well-armed, bloodthirsty gangs who named themselves after Taras Bulba, a fictional Cossack warrior. (His story, invented in the nineteenth century by Gogol and later portrayed in a Hollywood film starring Yul Brynner, was set during the ferocious Ukrainian rebellion against Polish rule in the late 1500s.) In the early 1940s, the Bulbutzye, tied closely to the Orthodox Church, felt an affinity with Hitler, who they thought would reward them with Ukrainian statehood. They savagely battled the Soviet partisans, assaulted ethnic Poles, and hunted down Jewish refugees. Because they knew the forest well, the Bulbutzye were actually more threatening than the Germans.

In an environment growing more treacherous by the hour, who would now grant us asylum? We went to sleep frightened and depressed.

In the early morning, mother awoke and told us in detail of a secluded little house that had come to her in a vivid dream. I don't know if Hershel was humoring her or not, but he said her description reminded him of a place he knew and he would lead us there. Through the bone-chilling night we hiked fifteen or twenty kilometers deeper into the forest, its trees long bare of leaves. My dejection grew with every step we took away from our friend Tichon. We passed some tiny hamlets along the way and I envied their residents—people with a place to live! I was even jealous of the farm dogs that terrified us with their howling—they had houses too. I wished God had created me as a canine. Or maybe as a bird that could just fly away.

Famished, freezing, and exhausted, we finally reached a decrepit one-room wooden dwelling in a remote corner of the forest. Hershel knocked on the door, and a woman appeared. I couldn't tell her age because she had a wizened face and only a couple of teeth, but she seemed to be the mother of five children, some of them very young, whom we saw behind her. She introduced herself as the Widow Yevdoshka, and warily let us in.

It was the first time I had entered a house in almost half a year, and I was nearly overcome by the sudden spike in temperature. Although Yevdoshka may have had enough wood for her oven that night, she lacked a lot else. One glance around her place revealed that her large family was dirt-poor. She couldn't part with a scrap of food but told us we could stay in the hayloft of her plain, thatch-roofed barn.

It was paradise. In the open attic, accessible by ladder, we had a wood floor, a real roof and walls, and as much hay and straw as we needed. We slept in the hayloft but went down to the barn's ground floor to use a bucket for human waste. Those trips scared me because of the farm animals. Among the pigs and chickens were two horned cows that seemed a lot more ornery than the docile cow that mother had kept in the backyard of our house on Chelmska Street.

I was soothed, though, by the comforts we now enjoyed and heartened by the reawakening of the land at winter's end: the first shoots of greenery through the snow, the first chirps of songbirds overhead. In March 1943, nothing gave me more hope than the coming of spring.

While I spent most of my time in the hayloft resting and recuperating from the ordeal of the forest, my father and uncle went out many nights to beg for grain or steal it from any unlocked barns or stables they could find. They returned weary after plodding through fields still deep with snow. Usually they brought back two sacks each, hung on their bodies, front and back, and filled with wheat and corn. The next night, near the barn, they'd grind the grain into flour by hand, turning an ancient mill made of two large stones. Then my mother prepared the dough and baked it in Yevdoshka's oven.

So we made loaves of bread—treasures—and yet we ate little of it. We subsisted mainly on potatoes as we did in the forest, and some eggs. Nearly all the bread, while it was still warm, was devoured by Yevdoshka and her hungry brood. It may be that she sold or bartered some of it as well. Without anyone actually explaining it to me, I could see that the grain for which my father and uncle risked their lives was the "rent" we paid for our lodging. The widow put herself and her children in great peril by harboring us; we provided her something valuable in return.

It was a fair arrangement, and we were even more grateful for it late one night when Tateh and Hershel returned from a food-foraging expedition, visibly shaken. Entering a barn, they'd found a Jewish family of six we knew well from Luboml, the Goldenzons, in the process of starving to death. Before the war Mrs. Goldenzon would frequently have tea and cookies in my mother's kitchen. Now she and her family lay together in a row, the living mixed in among the dead.

My father and uncle brought water and potatoes to those still breathing and tried to resuscitate them, but, with their bellies swollen and their eyes bulging, it was too late. Only medical attention could have saved them, and of course that was out of the question. Nor could the dead be buried; outside the barn the ground was frozen solid.

After about a month at Yevdoshka's she informed us that our sanctuary was about to become unsafe. With the spring thaw the peasants would soon be taking their cattle out to graze in the adjacent pastures, and we might be spotted.

Yet again Tichon came to our aid. We had previously seen him only once at Yevdoshka's. The widow had sent one of her kids to let him know our hideout's location, and he'd ridden out one Sunday to check on us and bring us some food. Now that we were forced to evacuate, he arrived again, this time with startling news: He had learned of a Soviet partisan brigade operating about ten kilometers away and thought we had a chance of joining it. If they had been Polish partisans we'd almost certainly be rejected; if Ukrainians, we'd likely be shot on the spot. But the pro-Soviet partisans might take in Jewish fugitives, he said, possibly even those without guns.

What choice did we have but once more to gamble with our lives? We told Tichon to set up a rendezvous and tearfully hugged him goodbye. My legs were wobbly from being cooped up in the hayloft for so long but I was able to move on.

A few days later, at great risk to herself, Yevdoshka drove us away in a horse and wagon and dropped us off at a prearranged spot, a little clearing hidden from the road. We felt nowhere near the affection toward her that we had for Tichon, but as we watched the widow leave we knew she genuinely wished us well.

Tense with anticipation, we waited for hours in the chilly spring air. Finally a man approached us in a military shirt and with a pistol in a holster on his belt. On his cap we could make out a red star.

5 | FIGHTING BACK

THE PARTISAN BATTALION'S POLITICAL OFFICER, the Politruk, dismounted and looked us over, four malnourished wretches with long, filthy hair. I could tell he was disappointed. "How many Germans have you killed?" he asked us in Russian. Our silence answered his question. "Let's see your weapons," he said next. Of course we had none.

I was sure we'd be rejected. But as soon as Uncle Hershel began relating his experience as a scout in the Polish Army and his vast knowledge of the region, the Politruk showed interest. He told us to follow him through the trees to the camp. We would no longer have to face the forbidding forest on our own.

Walking over ground that had barely begun to thaw, we soon reached another world, an independent city-state, it seemed, right in the midst of Nazi-occupied Ukraine. Dozens of people moved about freely, cooking, baking, and laundering. We went past tailors and shoemakers, nurses and a doctor. The camp hummed with the sort of human activity I hadn't known in years. But most startling were the rifles in the hands of young men dedicated to fighting the Germans. Armed resistance, only a faint idea in my mind before, was now a reality, and I was thrilled to be part of it.

Registration was simple: In the open air, a man holding a notebook briefly queried each of us and recorded our responses. When I gave my name as Sarah, he shook his head in disapproval. "Here, there are no Sarahs," he stated. "You will be called Sonia," and he wrote that down. I couldn't object and wasn't even sure I wanted to. I already felt like a changed person, and the new Russian name fit my new life.

Later in the day, after we washed and ate, I found out that this refuge had a dark side, too. Without my parents or Hershel, I was ushered into the log cabin of our battalion commander, a burly Belorussian named Popov, who always seemed like a teddy bear to me. He had to leave right away, but his wife sat me down for a serious talk. "Men far outnumber women here," she counseled me, "so don't waste any time, choose one of the fighters," and then she paused for emphasis, "as a special friend. He should be a strong guy, or an officer. You'll see things will go better for you."

My mouth fell open in shock. I was almost eighteen but wasn't ready for an intimate relationship, and certainly not in such forced circumstances. I didn't even know the facts of life. And my family was in the camp, too. How would they react to such a coupling out of necessity? But if I remained single, would I be vulnerable to sexual assault? Had I entered an oasis of freedom or a new kind of tyranny?

That evening my fears were greatly relieved. The kind Popov assigned my family its own tent. My parents and uncle would be my protectors; I wouldn't be beholden to some stranger.

I was lucky in this respect, but many other young women—in our battalion and throughout the entire partisan network—had a different fate. There was much sexual harassment and even rape, and for that reason single females did tend to pick a defender, often a brawny laborer, the sort of person with whom they likely would have had no contact before the war. Not infrequently a refined middle class Jewish girl would end up with an uneducated, hard-drinking Slav. I found out later that many of these unlikely liaisons lasted long after the war. The intense partisan experience bonded an odd couple together as little else could. But at the time I was horrified by the prospect.

In our camp, as in many others, sex was commonplace. There were unwanted pregnancies, and venereal disease was such a plague that one female carrier—seen going from tent to tent in the night—was "quarantined" for awhile in a kind of wooden cage. And an officer with VD was given some money by the commander and banished from camp until he was cured. Popov required weekly gynecological exams for every female except his wife, my mother, and me, a reassuring sign that we were considered "off-limits."

Our tent was a magnet for young men who wanted to *talk*, especially the two dozen or so Jews in the battalion of around a hundred. Only a few could squeeze into our small quarters, and one after the other they told us their stories; many were sole survivors of large families. They also talked politics, and the subject always seemed to be how long it would take America to invade Europe and establish a second front. When the Soviets air-dropped us cans of pork and beans stamped "Made in the USA," some of the guys took that as a sign of Uncle Sam's commitment to our cause.

Every night we tried to interpret the news bulletins that had been read to us that morning by the Politruk. Having earlier spent two years under Stalin, we knew that we were being fed a lot of propaganda, but after our long period of isolation in the ghetto and the forest, getting even such filtered information and discussing it with our new friends was highly stimulating. I learned about the German defeat at Stalingrad a few months earlier, and my hopes for an Allied victory rose.

One of our nightly visitors stirred another kind of feeling in me—as no one had before. Piotr Menaker, in his mid-twenties, which to me seemed quite mature, was a Jewish reconnaissance officer from far-off Vitebsk who had grown up with a love of Russian literature and folk music. A lieutenant in the Red Army, he had been captured by the Germans in 1941 but escaped from the POW camp, fled into the forest, and joined the partisans. Although not especially handsome, the skinny former accountant possessed an intelligence that shone through his eyes. He sure got my attention with a guitar dangling from his shoulder as he confidently rode his horse through the camp. He came into our tent almost every night and recited Pushkin's poetry and Tolstoy's prose and read his own flowery verse as well. He serenaded me with beautiful ballads. It was infatuating for an impressionable teenager who had just come out of the woods, where her only thoughts had been on survival and where she had seen but a handful of people for half a year. My eyes opened wide.

We lay on our stomachs and talked for hours during the warm "light nights" when the sun didn't go down until very late and the smells of the forest were sweet. But of course my parents were never more than a few feet away, and my mother in particular made sure there'd be no physical contact. As much as I basked in all the attention Piotr showered upon me, I wouldn't even think of disobeying her. Sure, I felt desire, but I was unwilling to disappoint Mameh and Tateh. "He's a nice boy, and maybe you'll marry him some day," she said in the same tone as if we had been back in Luboml, living normally, "but for now you have to be on your best behavior." She even told Piotr that she'd approve of a wedding after the war. She did allow me to accept his offer to *pretend* to be closer to me than he really was; we all thought that would discourage unwanted sexual advances from others.

Piotr's suggestion was prompted by an incident involving a demolition specialist named Grisha, a good-looking Russian, who had presented me a fine pearl-handled knife. When I turned it down—I didn't need it and certainly didn't want to be obligated to him—he retorted that I'd refused it because he wasn't Jewish. Now I'm in deep trouble, I thought, especially because the dyna-miters considered themselves the lords of the camp; nothing was

Volhynia in German-occupied Ukraine, 1942-43.
The Fyodorov Brigade operated north of the Kovel-Sarny railway line.

denied them. But Mameh saw a way out of it: "Accept the knife," she said. "Then we'll return the favor by knitting him socks." Her strategy, combined with Piotr's, worked well, and Grisha eventually became a trusted friend. And trust was vital in the partisans because our lives depended upon one another.

Our battalion was one of twelve in the Fyodorov-Chernigovsky brigade, named for its valiant leader, Alexei Fyodorov. In 1941, he had organized an underground movement against the Nazi occupation in eastern Ukraine near his hometown of Chernigov. The following year the Kremlin dispatched him to the forests of northern Volhynia to mold a unified force from the various factions opposing Hitler. Whipping the partisans into shape was a high priority for Moscow: Fyodorov was given the rank of Major General and was one of only about a hundred individuals to receive the accolade of Hero of the Soviet Union, not once, but twice.

His otriad, as partisan brigades were known, grew to almost 1,800 and severely crippled the German war effort by blowing up trains and disrupting the flow of men and materiel to the Eastern front. Like a half dozen other pro-Soviet otriads in the province, our core was composed of former Red Army men who, after being routed by the Wehrmacht in mid-1941, had gone into hiding or, like Piotr Menaker, had been captured and then broken out of German POW camps. A mixed group that even included some Uzbeks, Kazaks, and Tajiks, the Soviet veterans were joined by a variety of locals: anti-fascist Poles, Ukrainians, Belorussians, and Jews like us who had survived the liquidation of the ghettos in the fall of 1942 by fleeing to the forest. In such a diverse medley of people, all trying to survive under harsh conditions, ethnic and religious infighting could have ruined everything.

The iron hand of Fyodorov and his battalion commanders helped keep a lid on things. We were extremely fortunate that

A partisan demonstrates how mines were placed under railroad tracks.
(Courtesy YIVO Institute for Jewish Research, New York)

Popov was good to us, but we would have obeyed his orders in any case; we did as we were told. Uncle Hershel went out on missions, of course; we weren't that far from his native village of Nudyze, and he knew the lay of the land far better than anyone else did. My father served in a capacity almost as dangerous: food-foraging. With a few other men, he'd raid the surrounding farms and estates and, at gunpoint if necessary, demand livestock, canned goods, and, in the summertime, fresh produce. It was the only way the battalion could be fed. There were a handful of female fighters, but my mother and I usually stayed in camp, where we worked as assistant medics and as cooks. I had little experience in both of those areas, but I learned fast.

It was no easy task preparing food for our *rota*, or company, of 35, about a third of the battalion. We were among about half a dozen women gathering wood and then chopping it for a fire, searching for fresh water and then hauling it into the camp. Next we'd prepare hearty soup in huge cauldrons, containing potatoes and lots of meat. As when we were in the forest on our own, my family didn't eat the unkosher meat. We'd remove the chunks from our bowls and throw them out or give them away, crazy as that may sound to someone who is not an Orthodox Jew. Using a big frying pan with a long handle, I'd also bake round, seasoned flat breads, *pletzlach,* as we'd called the staple in Yiddish, or *lipyotshki,* as we now referred to them in Russian. We needed seventy of them so each person could be served two. All of this had to be done daily before the fighters returned.

Early on I was also sent on a mission—to blow up the train tracks near Luboml. This was a section of the vital rail line running through Kovel, across northern Volhynia and then all the way to Kiev. Throughout 1943, we and other partisans bombed these tracks almost daily. I was not given the task of actually planting the mine; I didn't even carry a gun. My job was to help provide first aid if needed. But I knew my life was in danger when I was given a long, gray military blouse with two pockets, each for a hand grenade—one for the enemy and the other to use on myself if I were about to be captured.

Our unit of about twenty—much larger than most partisan teams—accomplished its objective and derailed a long German train. Somehow the danger didn't frighten me. I was so elated finally to be fighting the Nazis that I didn't fear death. On the way back, the Bulbutzye, the Ukrainian nationalists, shot at us, and I barely lowered my head. If I die now, I thought, I'd have fallen as a fighter, not at the hands of some Nazi executioner thinking Jews were unworthy of life. This defiant attitude would not last forever—there were times when I was terrified and did all I could to protect myself—but initially I gave little thought to my personal safety.

Uncle Hershel took no precautions at all, and the other partisans remarked upon his bravery in battle. Of course, like many other Jewish fighters he had a tremendous score to settle and nothing more to lose: His wife and two little children had been killed. Now that he had brought my parents and me to a safe haven, he must have felt that he had reached the goal he'd set for himself when we met him in front of that farmhouse near Nudyze six months earlier.

All of this flashed through my mind when, less than two weeks after we joined the partisans, we learned of Hershel's death. Returning from a mission, his unit had been ambushed by the Bulbutzye. We were told that Hershel, already wounded, attempted to take out a machine-gun nest even though his comrades had implored him to lay low.

We heard all this from Popov at the entrance to the camp where we had hurriedly gathered with many others to welcome back the fighters. Mother immediately went to pieces. Slipping from father's grasp, she fell to her knees, lost consciousness for a while, and then wailed at the top of her voice. But the commander would permit no public display of grief. "Your brother died as a hero," he declared, "and we don't cry here. There will be no more tears." Mameh went mute, and while Popov's words burdened her in one sense, they may also have provided some comfort. At least we were informed of the precise location of Hershel's temporary gravesite. After the liberation my father would find that spot, retrieve his brother-in-law's body, and re-inter it in the Jewish cemetery of Luboml.

I, too, was shattered by the death of my uncle. But I also worried about what would now happen to the three of us whose lives he had saved. Would we be kicked out of the partisan camp? After all, we had been accepted based on Hershel's skills as a scout. With him gone, why would they continue to shelter and feed us? So even though I was torn up inside, I did my best to show an impassive face to Popov.

For I knew there were plenty of doubts about whether we'd fit into the partisan culture. I was too young to go out on most combat missions, and my parents too old. We rarely drank vodka or used vulgar language, and we sang and danced less than the others, many of whom reveled late into the night. Beyond that, we felt undercurrents of anti-Semitism and heard rumors—which my father believed—that some Jewish fighters who had not returned to camp had been shot in the back by other partisans. I never found out the truth of that horrible accusation, but research conducted after the war revealed that in some Soviet otriads murders of Jews committed under the cloak of enemy or friendly fire had indeed occurred.

An incident only days after our arrival underscored our sense of being outsiders. One of the battalion's operations had gone awry because the Germans had been tipped off by a Ukrainian peasant. So the "tongue," as we called such informers, was abducted by some of our fighters and brought into camp. After he was interrogated by Popov and his top deputies, he was turned over to the most hardened guys, the demolition team. I looked on as they tied him up and proceeded to club him furiously with heavy tree limbs. But that was just the beginning. One of them unsheathed his hunting knife, cut open the flesh in the captive's buttocks, and literally rubbed salt in the wounds.

Because the four of us happened to be there, we were expected to participate in the torture. Instead, appalled by the butchery of a human being, we backed away. Even Hershel, with all that he had endured, could not bear to watch. Then the name-calling started: "You weak Jews, you cowards, you don't know how to take revenge." In fact, my father would avenge his loved ones, but it would be a few years later and in a different way. For now, we were considered half-hearted warriors.

But Hershel's exploits and our stoic demeanor after his death dispelled the suspicions and we gradually felt more secure. By late June, though, we were engulfed by another tragedy. Our battalion was joined by a small band of independent partisans, almost all of them Jews. We rejoiced when they entered the camp until my mother noticed one of them wearing my brother Meir's jacket. It turned out this was the group with whom Meir had escaped into the Shatsk Forest just a few days before Luboml was liquidated! Now came the news we had dreaded: he had been killed in a firefight with the Germans. Meir, the liveliest one of us all, the one who made us laugh, and the one who we always thought had the best chance of surviving, was gone.

Again, we had to hold our emotions in check. We even had to stick to our routine and complete the day's work assignments as if nothing had happened. But when we were alone in our tent I saw Tateh collapse; there is nothing in the world worse than the loss of a child, and now he was hit a second time. Yet he was the kind of person who could keep even that excruciating pain inside him. He rarely talked about Meir, and if he recited Kaddish he said it privately.

I worried more about my mother. With her younger son taken from her so soon after the loss of her beloved brother, and only a year after Shneyer's death, she barely had the will to continue living. For days she wouldn't speak at all. While mired in my own grief for Meir, I gently reminded Mameh that I was her child, too, and I needed her. Somehow she summoned the strength to carry on.

Soon after we learned of Meir's death, our battalion pulled up stakes and made its way about seventy-five kilometers north-east to a new location deep in the Lubieshov Forest near the Belorussian border. Here we would unite with the other eleven battalions of the Fyodorov-Chernigovsky brigade, prepare for the cold weather ahead, and be in position to aid the advancing Red Army.

Only in our winter camp could I fully grasp the "forest republic" that the partisans had created. We no longer slept in tents but rather in sturdy wooden *ziemlankas*, camouflaged, insulated, and heated. My family had its own corner in one of the long, narrow cabins, half-buried in the earth and barely visible from a distance. Lice, which had caused us such distress when we were on our own the past winter, were no longer a major problem. Obviously, conditions were far from ideal, but I felt healthier and stronger than at any time in my life.

As the days grew chillier, provisions became harder to obtain, but raids into the surrounding villages—hamlets with names like Glusha-Mala, Glusha-Velka, and Kochotske-Vola—yielded cows and beans, fur coats and winter boots. One of our battalions, named for the legendary Polish Communist Wanda Wasilewska, cared for over a hundred noncombatants, including small children, in a civilian camp in the woods not far from us. They were not Jews, but rather ethnic Poles, who the vicious Ukrainian nationalists had targeted for death. Jewish civilians, too, were kept alive by Soviet partisan groups elsewhere in Volhynia, and even more so in Belorussia and Lithuania. Fed, clothed, sheltered, and defended, most of the refugees survived the war.

The winter camp even had a hospital, and my mother and I frequently worked there for the same good-hearted Russian Jewish doctor we had served in the spring. The infirmary occupied an entire tin-roofed house. It had been the largest dwelling in a nearby village and was lifted off its foundations and rolled on logs into the camp. Since there was a chronic shortage of medicine, we tried to use the herbal remedies abundant in the forest. Medical supplies ran low as well, and I had to wash used bandages in order to bind the wounds of the next injured fighter. Some of the patients in critical condition were returned to Russia in the same small Soviet planes that brought us guns and explosives.

Perhaps most impressive was the military parade I witnessed

in 1943 to mark the anniversary of the October Revolution. We were behind German lines and yet able to stage an elaborate production. Leading Soviet dignitaries were flown in and sat in a grandstand (I have no idea how it was assembled) to review "the troops." The fighters of all twelve battalions marched in military formation carrying their weapons and flags. It was a stirring sight and raised our morale enormously. I reminded myself that the Soviets, despite their repugnant political system, had saved us from the Nazis in 1939 and now were rescuing us again.

But fear of a German raid soon caused us to abandon the winter camp on short notice and trek farther east across the Styr River. I worried that my mother might not bear up under the rigors of such a journey. She had been worn down for years: by the affliction of the ghetto, the ordeal of the forest, and now the stress of partisan life. Worst, of course, were the shocks of losing her loved ones. She had shed so much weight that the speckled green dress she had worn before the war was now twice her size; she could wind the loose fabric completely around her waist.

The sixty-kilometer journey lasted twenty-four hours and took us through bogs and marshland. Until it froze, that spongy terrain would protect us from German motorized vehicles, but it sometimes proved treacherous for us, too. Our horse-drawn wagons frequently got stuck in the black muck and often we couldn't even extricate our shoes. I was in despair, but an encouraging word from Grisha, of all people, helped lift my spirits. "You'll see, one day you'll not only walk on a good road, you'll ride in your own automobile," something that seemed like wild fantasy when I was knee-deep in the wetlands of Volhynia in 1943. Grisha did not survive, but his line often comes back to me when I drive on the California freeways.

Unfortunately, another partisan made things tougher for us, especially for my mother. He was a top officer, a Jew named

Rescin, whom I had also rebuffed. After the danger of a German attack had passed and we turned around and headed back to the winter camp, he retaliated against all three Shainwalds by refusing to let us ride in the wagons even when the roads were dry and the horses had no trouble pulling their loads. My bone-weary mother had to trudge alongside half-empty carts just because of Rescin's spitefulness. I was utterly exhausted myself toward the end of the march and draped my body over a horse-drawn cannon for the final few kilometers. That was the most he would allow us despite the pleading of the doctor for whom my mother and I worked. None of us thought we could involve battalion commander Popov in the dispute. Thankfully we all made it "home."

I continued to spend a lot of time with Piotr. Once, about a dozen of us, including Popov, went on an overnight mission to search for food. This was one of the first times I was away from my parents. Piotr, naturally concerned that I'd become the target of one of our lecherous comrades, stayed close to me during the day. When it was time to go to sleep, our whole group crowded into a one-room farmhouse. Piotr told me we ought to lie down close together so there'd be no confusion about who was my partner for the night. I trusted him enough to know he wouldn't take advantage of the situation but I worried what my parents would think if they learned I'd "slept" with Piotr. Of course, just flopping down among the other men was a much riskier alternative, so I followed Piotr's lead and lay down next to him. Everyone was fully clothed—that was how partisans spent the night so they could make a quick getaway if necessary—but I still felt I was in a compromising position. Then I looked up and saw we had a chaperone, my father's closest friend in the battalion, a man about his age named Trachtenberg, who was stretched out right near us. I think he slept with one eye open the whole night. Piotr never touched me and my folks got a good report. I was glad that nothing happened for another reason: Who could think of romance in a room packed with so many people? The air was so musty it was hard enough just to breathe.

By the late fall we had been with the partisans half a year, and I was now well past eighteen. Some of the Russian women felt that my workload was too light and complained to Popov, who assigned me to the sanitation unit. Animals were slaughtered in a nearby village, and the parts we didn't cook, like the entrails, had to be buried deep in the ground. This was a health issue, of course, and perhaps that was why it made sense that as the doctor's assistant, I should be involved. But it was also a security concern, since any outsider coming across fresh-cut remains would surely suspect an encampment nearby.

No fewer than thirty men were entrusted with this three-day task, and my job, along with another woman, was to supervise the digging. But they didn't go down far enough—it was back-breaking labor shoveling the hard earth on cold mornings—and some cow udders and pig intestines poked up through the soil. The other woman and I knew it was wrong to leave it that way, but we didn't feel we could stand up to all those guys and insist they keep toiling. So we watched while the men simply covered up the whole mess with snow and we all figured it would remain concealed for many months, by which time our brigade might no longer be in the vicinity.

I didn't count on some unseasonably warm days that melted the snow and revealed the shoddy work. Even the gentle Popov was angry about my negligence as an overseer, although the punishment he meted out was mild by partisan standards: I was required to perform eight hours of guard duty, another burden I'd been spared up to this point, and would have to start with a four-hour nightshift.

I was issued a rifle and shown how to use it, but because

ammunition was so precious, no practice rounds were fired. The weapon was heavy and awkward in my hands, but I tried to get used to it. Then I was given the password and, at midnight, sent on my way to the perimeter of the camp.

The signal that night was the number 30. But our system was not simply to ask an approaching person to say the word. Instead, the guard would pick a number at random below 30—for instance, 10—and then the stranger would have to give the balance, 20. It was an easily decipherable code, but at least it prevented the password itself from being overheard by an enemy lurking in the black woods.

After about two hours on the first night, shivering and scared, I heard the crunch of footsteps in the distance. I called out 15 and the reply was not a number at all but "Popov." The commander himself had broken the rules and not responded properly. Did he still think of me as a child and not a real partisan? Was this some kind of a test? For a moment I considered firing in that direction—that's what I had been instructed to do. "I don't know 'Popov'" I shouted. Then I raised and cocked the rifle, hoping he'd hear the sound of metal on metal and know I was serious. Immediately, he answered, "15," and I lowered the weapon. He had come to relieve me two hours before the shift was supposed to end. "Warm up and get some sleep," he said with a grin.

If I was coddled at times, it all ended in early 1944 when, to my parents' dismay, I was sent into one of the bloodiest battles of the entire war. By now, the Fyodorov brigade had reached a new level: After more than a year as hit-and-run guerrillas, we now joined forces with the regular Red Army to confront the Wehrmacht.

Soviet infantry and tanks had entered northeastern Volhynia in January and pushed the enemy out of most of the province in a few weeks. This drive was the "tip of the spear" of Stalin's massive counteroffensive. The Germans, though, made a long and determined stand at the city of Kovel, the key railway junction astride the Turya River. There the two titanic armies threw everything they had at one another.

Our objective was to harass the Germans from the rear while the Red Army attacked along the front. With hundreds of fighters from our brigade, I left the security of the winter camp and rode on horseback to the edge of the inferno.

I remained for ten days. Except for the hiding place in Luboml, it was the most awful test of physical and mental stamina in my whole life. Assisting the same doctor for whom my mother and I worked since we'd joined the partisans, I tried to comfort an endless stream of comrades. Day and night the injured were brought in by the wagonload to our inadequate little field clinic. I saw every manner of injury: limbs blown off, heads split open, vital organs punctured. And the worst of it was that there was little we could do. Medication and supplies ran out fast, and it became hard to perform any medical procedure without spreading infection. With no other option available to us, we had to use the same bandages over and over. Sometimes all we could provide were words of hope. Many of the otriad's best fighters died right before my eyes, and others who were still alive when they left our care could not have survived for long.

We were positioned in a birch grove only a few kilometers from the battlefield. With the trees bare, we were exposed to bombs ourselves. Enemy fighter planes strafed us and mortar shells landed nearby. The sounds from the front were terrifying: a relentless barrage of grenades, canons, and rockets roared through the cold air. Any minute, I thought, we could be blasted to bits or overrun by German troops.

But the doctor and I worked non-stop. We barely slept or washed, and I didn't change my clothes or remove my shoes the

*The Soviet partisan brigade of another Polish-Jewish female partisan,
photographer Faye Schulman, who appears lower right.
(Courtesy Faye Schulman,* A Partisan's Memoir, *Second Story Press, 1995)*

entire time. Lighting a fire would have given away our position, so
for a week and a half we lacked hot food and sustained ourselves
with rations of crackers and dried bread. Finally, there came a lull
in the fighting—although the slaughter at Kovel would not end
for many more months—and we returned to our base. When I
came back, my parents, who had been frantic about the prospect
of losing their only surviving child, were overjoyed. But it took
them a while to recognize me.

I was now given more responsibility. We fought many skir-
mishes with the Bulbutzye, and having proven myself at Kovel, I
was sent out to accompany the reconnaissance squad a few times.
I rode a horse bareback, holding his flanks with my thighs, and
after a while it felt natural.

Once when we were resting in a clearing, the leader of the
mission, an officer from Piotr's hometown of Vitebsk, took me
aside before he rode out with others to comb the area. Sensing
even greater peril than usual, he handed me a leather pouch

containing detailed maps and charts, personal letters and photo-graphs, and messages he wanted sent to his family in the event of his death. "A few of us are going to see what's out there now," he told me. "You stay here, and if I don't return, be sure all of these things go to the right places. And make sure you let my mother know how I died."

Within hours he was killed. The sole survivor of the team came back to where I was waiting and could barely manage to tell me what had happened: At first the small squad was exultant when approached by a dozen men on horseback wearing Soviet uniforms. But they were Bulbutzye in disguise. They opened fire, shot the partisan officer in the chest, and mowed down several other comrades as well. We sometimes used the same tactic—our fighters wore German uniforms on occasion to penetrate the enemy's defenses—and the uncertainty of not knowing who was who in the forest magnified the terror of that winter.

But by the spring of 1944 we knew that the Red Army was truly drawing near and that we'd soon be out of the Nazi net for the first time in almost three years. Yet in my very last days as a partisan, having already witnessed so much death and destruc-tion, I had to absorb one more blow: Piotr Menaker lost his life on a reconnaissance mission. Of course I can't be sure we would have married had he survived, but except for my family he was the person to whom I felt the closest in the partisans.

I could not properly mourn his death, however. Even after his passing I did not want my parents to learn the depths of my feelings toward him. And in the eyes of the other partisans, sorrow often seemed a sign of weakness. Did I have the right, I wondered, in the midst of this collective struggle for survival, to wallow in my own loss?

I did come away with something of Piotr that enabled me to grieve later. A dreamy, romantic soul, he penned many love poems in Russian when he was out on patrol. His missives were delivered to me by a comrade returning to camp before he did. I have kept two of Piotr's poems, the only items from the forest still in my possession. They are precious to me, and I have read them again and again in private moments during all the years that have passed. At one point I worried that the penciled script might fade, so I went over every word in my own hand. That he loved and protected me in the wilderness gave me comfort and strength later in my life.

On September 15, 1943, he set down his impression of our first nights together months earlier: "without words you let me understand that you fell in love with me in the same way I did with you."

Like the rest of us he was always aware that each day might

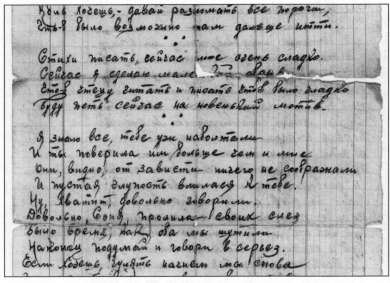

Piotr Menaker's love letter to me in the form of a poem
from the Lubieshov Forest, September 15, 1943.

be his last. "Take all...while the heart still breathes," he wrote. Perhaps that is the reason he was incredulous that Mameh would "block our way" or "obscure our path" as he put it, and expressed his frustration that he and I had not even kissed or hugged. Yet in his letters he fervently hoped that the Lubieshov forest would not be the end of our relationship.

The actual liberation—uniting with the Soviet forces and disbanding the Fyodorov brigade—was bittersweet, and not only because of the emptiness I felt knowing Piotr was dead. For one thing, I feared the breakup of the partisans would separate me from my parents, whom I couldn't bear to leave after everything we'd been through together. Because they were almost fifty years old, they were slated to be flown to Moscow and then relocated somewhere in the USSR. I could reunite with them after the war, but in the meantime I was expected to enlist in the Red Army as a regular soldier. Even with the carnage of Kovel fresh in my mind, I never thought of trying to dodge the draft. But I certainly wasn't looking forward to military service and I dreaded being apart from Mameh and Tateh.

A reprieve came, however, from an unexpected source: Rescin, the same officer who had harassed me and been so callous toward my mother on the march to the winter camp. Maybe he had feelings of guilt and now wanted to make amends. Or, because Piotr was gone, he was still trying to woo me and decided to switch tactics from the stick to the carrot.

Whatever the reason, his Jewish heart was finally moved by our plight, and he used his high rank and considerable influence to ensure my family would remain together in north-central Volhynia. We had no legal right to be in the province, but Rescin took official responsibility for our well-being and for me not enlisting in the army. He also arranged for us to be put up in a farmhouse. The owner's family would pay the highest price, Rescin told him, if we were harmed. Our new benefactor even put a horse and buggy at our disposal.

Before we left, we participated in a ceremony marking the end of our service with the partisans. No longer behind enemy lines, we assembled in an open field, and senior Red Army officers thanked us profusely for our sacrifices to the Motherland. Flags flew in the spring breeze. I did feel a new sense of freedom, yet it was not the exhilaration of someone who had survived a concentration camp or come out of hiding. For I was really liberated almost a year earlier, on my first day with the partisans.

6 | LOSS AND LONELINESS

OUR STAY IN THE PEASANT'S home, which Rescin arranged, did not last long. Hearing rumors that the Germans were mounting a counterattack and might re-conquer our region, we decided to flee east, deeper into the territory occupied by the Soviets. We loaded up our horse-drawn cart and traveled cautiously on the country roads. Even though we were supposed to have been liberated, we felt uprooted and unsafe again. Tateh felt he still needed to carry the handgun he had been issued in the partisans.

Along the way a number of other Jews came out from behind the trees, approached us, and walked alongside our wagon. Among them was a single man who had lost his wife and children, and another family of five still together. The oldest daughter was eighteen, like me.

Our group slept in barns each night and kept moving during the day. Soon we were all exhausted. My mother in particular was weak and run-down; the cumulative effect of everything she'd endured had finally caught up with her. Reaching a hamlet, we decided to rest for a few days in a one-room farmhouse; it had been deserted by its owners and was now occupied by a middle-aged Jewish man.

He was seriously sick—with typhus, we later learned—and lodging there proved a grave mistake. The infectious disease was widespread throughout east-central Europe in 1944 and 1945, in concentration camps, of course, but also in the countryside and cities. To this day I can't explain why we didn't move on—we had been familiar with typhus even before the war, and the danger of that dwelling should have been evident. But for once our survival instincts failed us and we allowed our weary bones to dictate our decision. The ailing man, barely intelligible, might be suffering from malnutrition, we told ourselves, and we fed him as best we could. Then my mother and I flopped down on a vacant bed in the middle of the room and closed our eyes. We barely noticed the lice.

Within a day the situation became horribly clear. The bed-ridden man passed away, and we learned from villagers that others had recently died in that house as well. By now, mother was too frail to be moved, so we had to remain there. In about a week she took a sharp turn for the worse, suffering from a very high fever, severe headaches, and extreme fatigue. She was so feeble she could no longer speak.

All I could think of was trying to work a miracle. In a reversal of roles, I went out seeking help and my father stayed behind at Mameh's bedside. After being in the partisans for a year, my Russian was better than Tateh's, and besides, I'd had experience as a doctor's assistant. We also thought that a woman would be less threatening to potential helpers.

With surprisingly little effort I found a Soviet partisan group nearby. They were sympathetic and, for a bottle of vodka I'd brought for this purpose, traded me medicine to strengthen her immune system. It needed to be administered by injection, and for that I arranged for a local *feldsher*, a kind of paramedic.

When he picked up her hand and found it turning blue he told me it was no use— we were just prolonging mother's life a short while. But even near the end her maternal feelings were still strong. I'd taken off my shoes that warm April day and was barefoot on the earthen floor. Dying and mute, mother nevertheless wanted to register her objection to my walking around that way. She pointed disapprovingly at my feet; it would turn out to be the last communication we would ever have.

Even as she faded away, I didn't give up. I wasn't as comfortable dealing with the Red Army as I was with the partisans, but I approached a Soviet platoon stationed at the other end of the little village, and among the soldiers was a woman doctor. I begged her to come back to the house with me and examine mother. She did, but there was not a glimmer of hope in her prognosis: "My child, we can't do a thing." Nonetheless, I made another run to the partisans for more medication and again got the feldsher to administer it.

There was no improvement. Soon we heard a horrid gurgling, for Mameh had lost the ability to swallow and every breath caused her respiratory secretions to vibrate loudly in her throat. I can hear it now, a raspy call that the end was at hand.

With that, all of my resolve cracked. First came disbelief: Given all we'd gone through together, how was it even possible to lose her this way, *after* the liberation? Then, unable to bear the noise of the death rattle anymore, I literally hid myself away. Curled up in a little nook behind the oven, I tried to shut out the world. I have no memory of what my father or the others were doing at that point.

Falling ill myself, I slipped in and out of consciousness. I can't recall mother's heart stopping and her body being removed from the house. I was too sick and too agitated to attend the small funeral my father arranged in a nearby village, and to this day I am not exactly sure where she was laid to rest.

But I do remember being alone in that house of death while the others were out burying her. Overwhelmed with loneliness, I went temporarily insane. She and I had been nearly inseparable during years of turmoil, and I knew that no one could fill her role, not even my father. I realized the excruciating pain her absence would cause for the rest of my life.

Screaming "I want to die too!" I ripped the linen off Mameh's and my bed and proceeded to wash it, seeking even more contact with the same germs that had destroyed her. Why *wash* the bed sheets? Maybe it was an attempt to mask my madness behind a domestic chore. If discovered, I would appear careless and even reckless, but not suicidal. Yet reflecting on it now, I can't deny I was trying to kill myself.

In fact, I exhibited the symptoms of typhus almost immediately although I had to have contracted it at least a week earlier, probably soon after we entered the house. Like mother, I had a high fever and couldn't get out of bed. Before long, my hair would fall out.

I was all that father had left now, and he knew I'd die without proper treatment. When someone told him of a Jewish pharmacist who had reopened his drugstore in a small town about thirty kilometers away, Tateh didn't hesitate. He carried me onto the cart and, joined by the other family and the single man traveling with us, we headed to Rafalovka.

Nearly all of the town's six hundred Jews had been liquidated in late August 1942, but their homes were now occupied by Ukrainians. We had to take up residence in an abandoned *shtiebel*, a one-room Jewish prayer house. There were no beds, so, sick as

I was, I lay on the floor with others. Our traveling companions, who mercifully never became infected, were kind to me, and the oldest daughter washed my hair and face every night and picked the lice out of my scalp.

But I would not have pulled through without the druggist Jacob Bass. He and his family had survived the mass murders almost two years earlier by fleeing into the forest and, like us, joining the Soviet partisans. His oldest son was killed on a mission, and his wife had died, too. Fortunately, he still had his younger son and daughter, David and Rivkele.

The handsome pharmacist was highly respected and influential in the town where his drugstore, on the main street, was vital to everyone's well-being. Immediately, Jacob Bass took a liking to my father and me as fellow partisans. Most of all, he wanted to help us as fellow Jews: Hardly any others were still alive in Rafalovka.

Not since Tichon had saved our lives in the forest did anyone do as much for us. His first goal was my recovery and he not only dispensed the medicine I needed, but also arranged for a feldsher to give the injections and for a doctor to treat me and monitor my progress. Beyond that, Bass instructed his housekeeper to cook food for us every day and deliver it to the shtiebel.

He also helped my father. At this late point in the war all able-bodied men were subject to the draft, including Tateh. Even though he had been spared conscription a month earlier because he was deep into middle age, a recruiting officer in Rafalovka ruled otherwise. Only Bass's intervention prevented our family of two from being torn apart at that awful time. Father had to hand over his revolver as a bribe to a Soviet official, a small price to pay for avoiding further hostilities and remaining with me.

I slowly got better, but I must have looked frightful. Because the front was not far from us, Rafalovka was still under German bombardment, and we often had to evacuate the shtiebel and find shelter in nearby cellars or in the woods. I could barely move, so my father and the single man in our group lifted me up and carried me to safety. We heard passersby in the street murmur, "Who is that old lady?"

As I regained my strength, I became more and more involved with the Bass family. David, a slender, brown-haired boy about my age, frequently came over to the shtiebel to check on me and before long we became enamored of one another. He was nothing like the mature, well-educated reconnaissance officer Piotr Menaker, who had been killed only a few months earlier. But the good-looking David had his own charms. He opened his heart to me, and we spoke intimately of life before the war, of the partisan experience, and of our families.

I was ill and lonely, grieving and depressed, and David proved to be a tonic for my wounded soul. He offered me love when I needed it most, and I returned his tender hugs and kisses. I also tried to comfort and help him with his problems. For one thing, he and his sister were upset that their father, Jacob, was about to marry their dead brother's fiancée, although they realized that in wartime unlikely matches frequently occurred. I could do nothing more than listen sympathetically to the misgivings David voiced, but in another family crisis, I was actually able to do some good. Young Rivkele Bass was going around with some of the Soviet officers based in Rafalovka, and both Jacob and David asked me to act like a big sister and teach her right from wrong. I did so gladly and think I influenced her a bit. It was a small favor compared to what the Bass family was doing for my father and me.

When I was fully recovered, Jacob took me aside and advised me to think of my future. "You'll need some job skills," he said, given that the Soviet Union was annexing the province of Volhynia. "Everyone will have to work, and you better prepare for that now."

He was well connected to the fast-emerging Soviet bureaucracy in our region and arranged for me to become an employee of the postal system. It may not sound like the opportunity of a lifetime, but in war-torn Eastern Europe the prospect of any career filled me with hope and anticipation. I soon left for a month-long training course conducted in the city of Rovno, an industrial hub and the provincial capital. Room and board was paid by the state, and Jacob sent me money for incidentals. When I returned I was given an entry-level placement as a clerk in the Rafalovka post office, the first real job I'd ever had.

But I only worked there for a few weeks. By late summer my father and I felt compelled to return to Luboml. With the Germans finally pushed across the Bug River in July, it became possible for us to make the hundred-kilometer train trip west from Rafalovka and go back home. I learned that the Allies had landed in Normandy and were driving across northeastern France. It was just a matter of time before the war would be over.

Was anyone from our large extended family still alive? Were any Jews left at all? What was the condition of our hometown? We feared the answers to these questions but had to find out. I didn't want to leave the Basses and especially David, but he would visit me there, I was sure.

Entering my beloved Luboml, I was overcome with an immeasurable emptiness that remained with me for the five months I spent there until the end of 1944. The void remains with me still. Yes, almost two years earlier we had had to crawl away like dogs in the middle of the night, and now we returned with our heads held high after proud service in the partisans. But the destruction of the town, the Jewish community, and nearly all of my loved ones blotted out any feelings of triumph I might have had.

The bitter truth was that even in defeat Hitler had achieved his goal of destroying us. My world had been broken in a thousand pieces, and I knew it could never be healed.

In the former Jewish quarter nearly every house lay in ruins from the great fire of 1941. One exception was the large home of my father's brother Simcha. Neither he nor his wife nor any of his four children had survived, and we fiercely felt entitled to live in their house on Chelmska, the same street where our own former dwelling had stood.

Of course, it was now occupied by Ukrainians. So the first night we slept nearby, in the home of a non-Jewish innkeeper we'd known before the war. He hid us away in his attic rather than in the rooming house proper. "It's for your own protection," he said, warning us about anti-Semitic attacks in the area. Indeed, surviving Jews were frequently met with brutality after the Holocaust, and my fear of our gentile neighbors would persist until I left Eastern Europe.

Still, as former partisans we enjoyed a high status, if not with the locals then at least with the occupying Soviet authorities. We went to the official in charge of housing and demanded to stay in Uncle Simcha's place. He wouldn't budge at first, but finally he relented. Two rooms were vacated and turned over to father and me. We regained at least a shred of continuity with our family's past.

But we found fewer than twenty Jews left in Luboml, about half of one percent of the prewar population. We had a tearful reunion with my friends Moishe and Pinie Lifshitz, who had come out of hiding a few weeks before we arrived. With them was a girl, my second cousin Chanah, whom Moishe would soon marry. We also met a few Jewish boys my age or a bit younger, schoolmates of mine who had fled before the liquidation of October 1942 and who had made their way back to Luboml: Avrum Getman, Natan

Sobel, Moishe Blumen, and Binyamin Perkal. They were all sole survivors.

Father, due to his knowledge of the surrounding villages and his good relations with the Soviets, was quickly tapped for a government job. He directed a team of ten men to find and purchase furs and hides, which were salted and then shipped to distribution centers throughout the USSR. Tateh made a point of hiring Jews but still had three open slots, which he filled with gentiles who had hidden Jews during the war, including one who had saved Moishe Lifshitz and his future wife.

The Soviets, meanwhile, were scouring Volhynia for workers of a different sort: They needed miners for the Donbas coalfields, hundreds of kilometers away at the other end of Ukraine. We all knew that it was the equivalent of a slave-labor camp, but we weren't sorry to see some of the Ukrainians who had collaborated with the Germans rounded up and shipped off to toil in those black pits.

Father and I were shocked, though, when our teenage friends Getman, Sobel, Blumen, and Perkal were slated for Donbas. The decree had been issued by a new regional official, an anti-Semite named Denisyuk. At no small risk to ourselves we went to his office to try to spare the boys from a horrible fate.

Only because we were former partisans did we have any chance to get him to reverse his decision. I held nothing back in confronting him. "Aren't you ashamed?" I asked. "Haven't those four youths already suffered enough? They should be going to school, not sentenced to the mines." He retorted that if we didn't mind our own business he'd send me to Donbas, too. But we angrily informed him we were prepared to go to his superiors. With four lives at stake, we felt it was worth trying to exert some pressure. A few days later we learned his order had been rescinded.

Father also reached out to help a young woman engaged to his nephew, who was thought to be deep in the Russian hinterland. Rochl Weisman, who had lived with us for a while in Luboml, was also put on the list for Donbas, by a native-born Ukrainian bureaucrat who was deaf to Tateh's objections. As it happened, the man had served in the Fyodorov partisan brigade, and father recalled having heard that he'd deserted while on a dangerous mission. That story, related to the Communist Party leader in Luboml, was all it took to get the Ukrainian removed from his post. Rochl was allowed to stay in town and was eventually reunited with her fiancé.

Tateh also used his influence to avenge the brutal slayings of his nephews Yidl and Meir back in 1942. They had fled to the forest from Aunt Tziril's crowded house just before the rest of us entered the hiding place. Once they reached the countryside, a peasant who coveted Yidl's suit shot them dead. Now father wanted the murderer to pay in blood for his deed.

Yet Jewish life was so cheap in those days that we all knew the accusation of merely killing two Jews on the run would not have any consequences. So father went to an officer he knew in the Red Army and charged the peasant with a fictional crime: having betrayed escaped Soviet POWs—army officers, no less—to the Germans. Several soldiers were dispatched to interrogate the man in his farmhouse, and as luck would have it they discovered an illicit cache of weapons in his barn. Now it was easy for them to assume him guilty of informing on their comrades as well. They bound his hands and feet and buried him alive in a deep earthen pit. Never have I had any qualms about father's act. It was the only way we could have gotten even an ounce of justice.

While Tateh was a powerful figure in post-liberation Luboml, I had a position of some authority, too: deputy director of the post office. We issued money orders and cashed checks as well, and part of my job was detecting forgeries by referring to a classified procedure manual, a task I took very seriously. I also worked as a clerk behind the counter and kept the account ledgers on the whole operation.

One day I was thrilled to see Tichon walk in. On top of everything else, the post office sold newspapers, and he had come in to buy a few, not to read but to cut up and use as rolling papers for his cigarettes. I excitedly motioned him to come to the front of the long line. How proud he was of me! When we'd first met in the woods less than two years earlier I was a terrified, unkempt, starving girl; now he saw me as a well-groomed, responsible young woman, contributing to society. I invited him to dinner, and he, his wife, and oldest daughter would visit us frequently over the next few months. It's not the most elegant adage, but a Yiddish saying expresses the gratitude I felt for him: "If I could, I would have washed his feet and then drank the water."

Father presented Tichon with a gift, a token of what we owed him for keeping us alive in the forest. We had little of value, but Uncle Hershel had left a kind of inheritance. Just before he and his family had been transferred to the ghetto, he had placed

A retouched studio photo of Tichon and his wife, Fedora.

much of his furniture with peasants for safekeeping. Tateh now retrieved a well-crafted armoire with an inlaid mirror, kitchen cabinets, a fine table and matching chairs, and other items and gave them to Tichon and his family.

What a rare stroke of good fortune it had been to have a protector like him. This was never clearer to me than when I had to work late into the night at the post office for a heartrending task. Dozens of inquiries poured into Luboml each week asking the whereabouts of people I knew had perished. These letters and postcards invariably came from family members of the missing person, and I couldn't bear to respond that their loved one was presumed dead. In any case we were required to write a formulaic reply, the equivalent of "address unknown," which I penned under the light of a kerosene lamp and personalized as best I could by adding a comforting line or two of my own. (At times I received an inquiry about someone's relative whom I'd known had survived, and later in America I was occasionally sought out and thanked for making the connection. But once, at a gathering in New York, a man came up and showed me one of those postcards I'd sent in 1944—the only thing left of his family. I was astonished when he gave it to me to keep. He'd carried it with him daily but, finally meeting the writer, he felt he could relinquish it.)

From my desk in the post office of just one devastated shtetl among the thousands, I was beginning to grasp the scale of what had befallen our people. Where was God when all this happened? When innocent children like Uncle Hershel's two kids were murdered? When saintly people like my mother died of disease? When dedicated rabbis like Moishe Shneyers were beaten to a pulp? When brave young men like my brothers never returned? I alternated between anger at God and doubt about his very existence.

Religious observance was now one of my lowest priorities. In

A postcard sent by Sonia from post-liberation Luboml, October 8, 1944, in Russian. The back of the card reads: "This is in answer to your letter. Your relatives whom you are asking about in your letter do not live in the city of Luboml anymore."

the ghetto and the forest it had often been impossible to practice Judaism, but now the reason was more a lack of will. Despite all my marvelous childhood memories of the Jewish festivals, when I returned to Luboml in 1944, I had no desire even to light the Sabbath candles on Friday evening.

Nothing could comfort me; I felt I was living in a cemetery. It tore me up to see the site of my family's home at 37 Chelmska Street, and I had to pass it four times a day, walking to and from work mornings and afternoons. In place of the attractive house and lovely garden was a vacant lot overgrown with weeds. In place of a warm family was cold silence. All that remained of that household was one cement step—the killers and the looters, the fire and the elements had swept everything else away.

That six-inch-high slab was the only *matseveh*, or tombstone, I had. Despite my pain, I paused there frequently and tried to visualize the faces of my mother and brothers. I talked out loud to them—about the partisans, David Bass, my new job.

How I could have used their advice and support as I struggled to make my way in the world! My salary was miserable, a mere 350 rubles a month, barely enough to purchase two pounds of butter. Father earned enough for the two of us to get by, and at work he had access to sacks of salt, which he could sell or barter. Unlike me, one of my colleagues in the post office, a single woman with a limp, had to survive on her own. I nearly cried when I saw what she could afford for lunch—a small bowl of watery soup. In desperation she stole a parcel and was caught. She was fired immediately, and we never heard from her again. God only knows what further punishment she received.

The director of the post office, a guy named Koslowski, was a lazy drunkard. He gave me virtually no guidance, and whenever I had a question he answered it with a Russian cliché that roughly translates as "six of one, half a dozen of the other." When the regional headquarters demanded reports on our productivity— and in the Soviet system the paperwork was endless—Koslowski simply made up numbers to show we'd met our quotas and encouraged me to do the same.

I kept the financial records accurately, however, so I was shocked when the comptroller from the main office in Lutsk came to town and claimed 70,000 rubles were missing! Koslowski actually defended me; he told the fellow of my father's high standing and that I'd be unlikely to risk everything by resorting to embezzlement. That didn't change the comptroller's mind, but at least he was willing to discuss the matter in my home over dinner. I quickly got him and Koslowski drunk, and my father and I found out the whole thing was a set-up. It still didn't remove the cloud from over my head, but a few weeks later, after a second "audit," he came to the conclusion that "only" 20,000 rubles were unaccounted for. Again I got them both drunk and received the promise of another review of the finances. After that, the problem shrank to 5,000 rubles. Only after a third such exercise did he finally admit that nothing was out of line.

The false accusation may well have been retaliation stemming from my father's and my openly expressed desire to leave the Soviet Union and move to Poland. Since the Bug River was now the international border (as it had been in the fall of 1939, when the Red Army seized the eastern half of the republic), in order to return to our homeland we had to leave our hometown.

It is not that we saw a future for ourselves in Poland. Rather, after all of the bloodletting we'd witnessed on the European continent, we longed to settle in Palestine or the West. But first we needed to break free from the prison of Stalinism, and crossing the Bug River was the initial step. Of course, Poland, too, was destined to be a Communist dictatorship and a satellite of Moscow, but in late 1944 we hardly felt that was inevitable. After all, Britain had gone to war over Poland, and we didn't think the English and the Americans would abandon it to the Soviets. We figured that a right-wing and possibly anti-Semitic faction could take control, but we simply assumed that whatever regime emerged, it would be less oppressive than was Stalin's totalitarianism. In any case, we thought of Poland as only a station along the way.

Koslowski didn't want me go. No doubt he realized that in my absence he'd actually have to do some work. He tried to scare me with stories about famine in Poland. "You'll need gold coins just to buy bread," he declared, "Do you have them?" To keep him at bay, I claimed it was just an extended visit to search for friends and relatives and that I'd be back. In truth, I didn't know what to expect in Poland, but if there was a chance to exit the USSR, I wanted to take it.

I might have felt differently about leaving the country if David Bass were still in my life. He did visit me twice in Luboml, and we spent wonderful days together, but then he vanished. My letters went unanswered, and my inquiries were in vain.

Only decades later, reuniting with the Basses in Israel, did I find out that the entire family was forced to sneak out of Rafalovka and the Soviet Union on a moment's notice. Due to a sudden shift in the political landscape, Jacob had fallen out of favor with the Party apparatus. He could no longer protect his son from the draft and feared even worse reprisals. The family was able to find sanctuary in Lublin, and David, one of the early recruits of the semi-secret Zionist network, *Brichah*, soon sailed for Haifa, where he joined the Jewish underground. Just weeks after his arrival he was killed in a firefight with Arabs.

In Luboml, I knew none of the reasons for his disappearance and naturally felt abandoned. Sometimes I even wished I were back with the partisans, where I'd had so many loyal comrades around. At nineteen, my prospects in Luboml looked darker and lonelier than ever.

The choice to leave was harder for my fifty-year-old father, who would be giving up a good position and embarking on a rough, uncertain road. We had no idea how we'd support ourselves. Yet when our visas arrived—and we were among the first Jews repatriated under a formal agreement between the two countries—we didn't think twice. We packed and headed to the train station.

Early on, we'd confided to Tichon and one of his daughters about our plans to emigrate. She too was deeply unhappy in the Soviet Union and begged to come with us. Once Tichon gave his approval, we agreed right away; how could we pass up an opportunity to do a good turn for that family? But, probably because she was an ethnic Ukrainian, she was denied a visa, even though,

like us, she was a former Polish citizen. (The second Polish republic, unlike the first, would have very few minorities. The Jews,
of course, had been decimated, many *Volksdeutche* were expelled,
and the Ukrainians were largely left east of the country's new
border.)

Father and I did have some traveling companions, however.
Our distant cousins Moishe and Mordche Meiterman and
Mordche's wife, two children, and sister had recently returned to
Luboml and were ready to join us, as was a single woman about
my mother's age named Zelda.

I was nervous as we all sat in the railway car and waited for
it to pull away from the station. Many of those who registered to
leave the Soviet Union for Poland in 1940, I recalled, were considered traitors and shipped off to Siberia instead. I was relieved
when the train headed due west and we quickly crossed the Bug.

However, we didn't go very far into Poland. Our destination was Chelm, the town we'd visited several times when I was
a child, only thirty-five kilometers from Luboml. We had some
friends there, and it seemed the safest place to begin this new
phase in our lives.

Chelm has been unfairly ridiculed in Jewish folklore as a
town of loveable morons, people whose twisted logic leads them
to the most ludicrous behavior. As one of a hundred legends of
Sholom Aleichem went: A Chelmer who had lost his eyeglasses in
the park looked for them in the street, under a lamppost. Why in
only that one spot? Because that's where the light was. I hoped
our short train ride to another country wasn't a similar example
of human folly. But it certainly began with a series of bad breaks.
All of my worldly possessions, including a pair of new shoes, were
crammed into a little suitcase—and stolen en route.

To make matters worse, it was raining hard when we arrived,
and none of us had any rain gear. We ran through the wet streets

looking for the house of Zelda's friends, the Dunietz family, and came in drenched. Understandably, they couldn't put up so many people for long, so we had to move to a communal shelter and take our meals in a soup kitchen. We finally found long-term lodging, but it was in a cramped attic, utterly lacking in appeal, which my father and I had to share with his distant cousin and that man's niece. The landlady lived in the attic too and felt entitled to eat our food whenever she wanted.

Father, meanwhile, with few options to earn a living, resorted to selling used clothing in the Chelm flea market. With another man, he traveled by train across Poland to Lodz and Breslau—dangerous journeys for Jews in those days—to obtain a stock of garments. I think they had belonged to the doomed Jews of those cities and were sold by the government for next to nothing.

It was pitiful to see him carrying bundles of those clothes up several flights of stairs to our attic, his face dripping with perspiration. I often helped him sell the second-hand pants and shirts in an outdoor stall, and I was so embarrassed by how low we'd fallen—selling *shmattehs* in the street—that I dreaded being discovered by anyone who had known us in our prewar, middle-class lives. Once I saw three Luboml-based Soviet soldiers I knew, and I ran away. Yet I was also aware that once we had made the decision to start over, there was no other choice but to begin at the bottom.

Before long I met other Jews in Chelm who had fled the Soviet Union. Most of them were of my generation, since few of the children or the elderly had survived, and we formed a loose friendship circle. One Friday evening, a married woman named Chanah Gitales and her sister knocked on our door and asked if I'd care to join them and some people new in town for a walk. I said yes, and then, with a knowing glance, she suggested I wear something "a little nicer" than the plain, navy blue knit dress I had on. "Sorry," I replied, "that's what I wore here from Luboml and that's all I have." Alright, she said, not wanting to keep the folks downstairs waiting any longer, "Let's just go."

7 | "Knight on a White Horse"

When Chanah, her sister, and I came down from the attic, a few young people were gathered outside, and we all started walking toward a prettier part of Chelm. It was late spring now and everything was in bloom. Right away, one of the men began talking earnestly to me, and before I knew it we had separated from the others and were engrossed in conversation.

Isaak Orbuch, thirty years of age, was a full decade older than me. Sturdy and broad-chested, he had an air of confidence and determination, "a bull of a man," people would say later. I quickly found out that his background had both similarities and differences with mine. Born in Yagodjin, a village not far from Luboml, his father died when Isaak was five, and his mother struggled to raise him and his two older sisters. Scrimping on almost everything else, she paid dearly for a *melamed* to ride out to the Orbuch house and tutor Isaak in the Mishnah and Gemorrah. When he grew older, he studied in a yeshiva in Luboml and would retain a knowledge and love of Talmud his entire life.

Yet the forceful Isaak was anything but a pallid *yeshiva-bocher*, as we called a boy with his head buried in the holy books; he was a man of action. As a youth he had been a leader of the right-wing Zionist youth group Betar; wearing his snappy uniform, he'd proudly participated in military drills and parades. In the late 1930s he served in the Polish army, but when the Soviets occupied Volhynia, he was drafted into the Red Army, spending six years in the armed services overall. Later in the war, he became a government agent buying up cotton throughout Soviet Asia. In that job, with precious identification papers enabling him to travel from town to town, he was able to trade goods and generate some extra money for himself. When I encountered him in Chelm he had a few valuable gold coins jingling in his pocket.

None of the Orbuch women survived the war, and Isaak came home in 1944 bereft and adrift. He was a bit of a nomad, flopping down in a different house every night with no place to leave his belongings. I sometimes saw him sheepishly carrying around a freshly washed shirt, still wet. He literally had nowhere to hang it up to dry.

This was a man who sorely needed a bride and I soon learned he had me high on his list of prospects. By coincidence, he had worked briefly under Koslowski in the Luboml post office in 1940, and when he returned to town after the liberation, our mutual former boss told him of a local girl, now believed to be in Chelm, who would make a good wife. "Bring her back here and we'll have a grand wedding," he said.

Isaak and I had actually met back in 1935, when I was only ten. He had come to Luboml to date a young woman, coincidentally named Sonia, who lived across the street from us, and for some reason I'd talked to him briefly at that time. We both recalled that, and reflecting upon on those prewar years—from another lifetime, it seemed—was poignant for both of us.

I didn't attach much significance to that twilight stroll we took in Chelm, but Isaak continued to visit me and soon became serious. I was flattered by the attention of an "older man" and appreciated the kindness he showed my father and me. But when he suggested marriage I was quite hesitant. Initially I wasn't as attracted to him as I'd been toward Piotr or David, and he hadn't yet touched my soul in the ways they had. Beyond that, my mind was still in turmoil over Mameh's death the spring before, and I didn't feel confident about making big decisions. When I did think about my future, I envisioned going back to school or trying in some other way to salvage a bit of the youth that the war had stolen from me.

On the other hand, I wasn't sure I could afford to let this opportunity slip away. Although barely twenty, I feared it could be my last chance because so many young Jewish men had just been killed. And my track record had been tragic: one man I

Isaak in Betar uniform before the war with his mother (seated), sisters, and brother-in-law.

might have married never returned from a partisan mission, and another fled his hometown without leaving a trace.

Then there was Rescin. He had tracked me down in Rafalovka and proposed to me while I was still sick. The former partisan officer had quickly landed an important job, manager of all the bakeries in the city of Kovel, but I could never think of marrying him; his behavior in the forest toward my family had been so erratic that I questioned his honesty and integrity. I now wondered whether I'd just had terrible luck with men or if something were really wrong with me. Either way, a marriage proposal might not come my way again.

I thought, too, about my dear father and how hard he toiled to support us both. If I had no job prospects myself, shouldn't I at least have a husband who could be a breadwinner and ease the burden? Most of all, I wanted to end the loneliness that had grown unbearable in the year since I'd left the partisans. Yes, I had Tateh, but I felt alone.

Here was probably the most important decision of my life, and I had no one to turn to for advice. My thoughts were confused, and I just couldn't make up my mind. I asked Isaak for more time to decide, but he made it clear he wouldn't wait long and gave me an ultimatum: I'd have a couple of weeks to think it over, and if I wasn't ready he'd move on to another town to continue his search.

During that period of indecision I left Chelm and accompanied my father on one of his business trips to Lodz, where I visited acquaintances and bought some needed commodities. Our impoverishment was never clearer. With the few zlotys Tateh could spare me to buy a suit, the only one I could afford in the open-air market had a jacket that was way too tight. I took it anyway and altered it by opening the seams and adding a differently colored piece of fabric. How much longer would I have to live this way? I asked myself.

One evening, in the home of a family from Luboml now transplanted to Lodz, I spoke about the choice I had to make. There were a lot of practical reasons for marrying Isaak, I explained, but I wasn't passionately in love with him. To them the right path was obvious, and they seemed annoyed at me for deliberating at all. "What are you waiting for," asked the lady of the house, raising her voice, "a knight on a white horse?" I had no answer for her.

Back in Chelm, only days before the deadline, I broached the subject with my father for the first time. "Isaak wants to get married," I informed him. "And do you?" he asked. I replied in the affirmative but softly and tentatively, my voice betraying all of the ambivalence I felt. Sadly, Tateh was unwilling or incapable of delving into the pros and cons of such a marriage. He didn't ask if I loved Isaak, if I wanted to have children with him, spend the rest of my life with him—nothing of the sort. The only advice Tateh gave me was to pick Rosh Chodesh, the first day of the month in the Hebrew calendar, for the wedding date. That way we wouldn't be required to fast as was otherwise the rule for the bride and groom. How I wished I could talk to Mameh or my brothers just one more time, but they were gone to me forever. Never did I feel their loss more.

Isaak's and my wedding took place on August 10, 1945 on a Friday evening before sundown. The preparations were daunting. I didn't know how to cook a grand dinner and we'd invited twenty or so guests—probably a high proportion of all the Jews in Chelm at that point. Of course, my attic apartment lacked a proper kitchen, to say nothing of a dining room. When I'd had Isaak over for supper, we'd eaten on a board placed over a barrel and I'd had to rely on our landlady's help when I wanted to prepare something special.

Our wedding picture, August 10, 1945 in Chelm.

Now I turned to the few married women among our friends. They made some of the traditional delicacies, like gefilte fish and sponge cake—for which I beat the egg whites in a wooden basin normally used for washing infants. The Meiterman brothers brought a big barrel of beer. We set up the *chuppah*, or bridal canopy, in the courtyard of our building—it couldn't fit into our narrow attic—but we had no rabbi to perform the ceremony. One of the men in our little circle officiated, which is permitted under Jewish law. Since I didn't have any kind of a wedding gown, I got married in a very simple print dress that I made from a piece of fabric Isaak had purchased for me. It was a garment so casual that I'd wear it routinely during the next few years.

Of course, it wasn't the threadbare surroundings but rather the trauma we'd all just been through that darkened the mood. None of the four siblings Isaak and I had between us, and only one of our four parents, would be there to share our joy. Nor were there any aunts, uncles, or first cousins. Yet two people joining together in matrimony so soon after the cataclysm was itself a cause for gladness, and I believe that everybody's spirits were raised that summer evening.

As our friends finally departed, I prepared mentally for my first night in bed with my husband. I was inexperienced and uninformed and didn't know what to expect. So I was nervous but also unsure if anything would happen at all. The plan was for Isaak to share my bed in the attic, but the four other people who lived there, including my father, would be in the same room with us! No one had raised the issue of privacy for the newlyweds, and I was far too shy to bring it up. It would have been great if we could have gone away on a honeymoon to a seaside resort, but in our circumstances that was about as likely as a trip to the moon.

As it turned out, the wedding night was anything but rapturous. With the lights out, Isaak lay down next to me—and his weight caused the flimsy bed to come crashing down with a momentous thud. Fortunately, neither of us was hurt, but it was quite embarrassing in front of the others—a mishap fit for the *shlimmazels,* or sad sacks, of Chelm. We had to sleep on the floor and, needless to say, the rest of the night was uneventful. Indeed, we would never be intimate in the presence of anyone else; the only time we could be alone would be an occasional afternoon for an hour or two when nobody else was around.

Yet all of the material hardships paled in comparison to the vulnerability we felt as Jews in the new Poland. Simply put, we were in constant fear of being assaulted or even killed by anti-Semites wherever we went. Our building was located in a dangerous place, opposite a Polish Army barracks, and the soldiers frequently taunted and accosted us in the street. Beyond that, I had the misfortune of being harassed by a Pole from Luboml who

Shortly after our wedding.

would get drunk, shoot his gun in the air under our windows, and demand I come down to meet him. He was actually stalking another Jewish Sonia whom he'd heard had moved to Chelm, and confused me with her, but the fact that it was a case of mistaken identity hardly calmed my fears.

The poisonous atmosphere in Chelm was hardly unusual. Attacks against returning survivors were prevalent throughout the whole country and every Jew we met was worried about physical security. We talked about little else at that time and I was not surprised to find out later that around 1,500 Jews were killed in Poland during the immediate postwar years.

Even before the end of hostilities, survivors in liberated

areas were often beaten in the streets or thrown off moving trains. Although the Nazis had murdered millions of Catholic Poles, the locals often borrowed the vocabulary they'd heard during the German occupation and shouted the words *Juden raus* at terrified Jewish men, women, and children. The authorities, even the increasingly powerful Communists, who had also suffered unspeakably under Hitler, did virtually nothing to protect us, perhaps because they wanted to curry favor with the bigoted masses. Complaints lodged by Jewish victims of violence were ignored, as were protests against the discrimination we faced when we tried to find jobs or housing.

The Poles, like the Ukrainians in Volhynia, had assisted the Nazis in killing Jews and had looted a staggering amount of Jewish property. Now that a tiny remnant of us had improbably returned from hell, we were a living reminder of those criminal acts—and a threat to lay claim to a house, business, or, in some instances, even a Jewish child hidden among non-Jews. "We thought you were all dead," was the constant refrain hurled at us in equal measure of incredulity and contempt.

We were targeted for other reasons, too. A good number of the highest officials were Jewish party members who had spent the war years in Moscow. The Poles now tied Bolshevism and Judaism together—*Zydokomuna,* or "Judeo-communism," they called it—and blamed us for the spread of Stalinism just as they had following the Soviet invasion in September 1939. On top of that, of course, was the wellspring of hatred emanating from the Catholic Church.

It all made for a perfect firestorm of oppression, and we were appalled at its fury. In June 1945, in the town of Rzeszow, barely a hundred kilometers from Chelm, a rabbi and other Jewish leaders were arrested by the police and accused of the ritual murder of a nine-year-old girl. They were eventually released, but not

before a riot against Jews that resulted in beatings and robber-
ies. Even more disturbing was an outrage in Krakow the day after
our wedding. Again, the medieval blood libel ignited a pogrom,
during which a mob stormed and plundered a synagogue, killed
several Jews, and seriously injured dozens more. Some of those
taken to the hospital were beaten a second time there. The worst
atrocity occurred almost a year later in the city of Kielce, where
a crowd, not merely unrestrained but actually *aided* by the police
and a Soviet military detachment, slaughtered scores of Jews.
But by then, thankfully, my family was already out of Poland.

Indeed, we left Chelm soon after I got married. We thought
another part of Poland might be safer and offer more opportunity—the so-called "recovered territories," a vast swath of German land ceded to Poland after the war to compensate for the
loss of the eastern half of the country to the Soviet Union. This
newly regained part of Poland ("recovered" because it had been
ruled by the Polish kings in the eighteenth century) was closer
to the west, and most of the Poles there were newcomers like we
were, transferred by the government as a counterweight to the
ethnic Germans.

Like a number of other Jews from eastern Poland, we settled
in the northwestern city of Szczecin, known until 1945 as Stettin,
a bustling Baltic port city near the mouth of the Oder, only a few
kilometers from what would soon become the German Demo-
cratic Republic, or East Germany. Without any down payment
we were able to take over a little grocery store and handsomely
furnished living quarters on the floor above. Its former owners
were Germans who, rather than live in what was now Poland, had
fled west.

The commercial hub, bombed heavily by the Allies, had lost
almost all its prewar charm. But our situation had improved
greatly compared with Chelm. True, my father and husband still

had to make the perilous train trip to Lodz to purchase the goods we sold. Even wearing Red Army uniforms (Isaak still had his old one) did not ensure a safe journey. They were once caught by the police and roughed up before their release.

But we felt the risk was worth taking. Our German-speaking customers in particular, who were mostly women, liked a pungent, sour milk cheese known as *harzer Kaese* and even in those difficult economic times it sold briskly. Business was good, and for the first time since we'd left Luboml we had a steady stream of income. We could even afford to employ a German housekeeper and her daughter, both of them happy to work for nothing more than three meals a day.

Just as I was beginning to feel a bit of stability, I had to absorb another shock that came from within my own family. One day, father returned from Lodz and matter-of-factly introduced me to his new wife. I was still adjusting to my own spouse and had no inkling Tateh was planning to get married and no advance notice before meeting my new stepmother. Only a year and a half had gone by since Mameh's death—too short an interval, I thought, for father to remarry. And then for him just to spring it on me like that!

Chava Siegel, from Dubienka, a village on the Bug River, was a few years younger than my father. Hidden by Seventh Day Adventists, she had survived the war, but her husband, daughter, and a son about my age had perished.

I could see she was decent, resourceful, and intelligent, but I deeply resented her. She asked me to call her "mother," and I flatly refused; the best I could do, I told her, was address her as aunt, *Mima* in Yiddish, which I shortened to *Mim*, and which everyone else started to call her, too. When she came into the store to help out, I turned my back on her; I couldn't accept that another woman was taking my real mother's place. At first, she and Tateh lived with us in the same apartment, but my chilly reaction caused them to move across the hall to their own place. Eventually I would come to love her and be grateful that my father could share the rest of his life with such a fine lady. But that would take quite a while.

In Szczecin, my new family of four suddenly came under a mortal threat. Our thriving little business had drawn the attention of some Polish gangsters. They hung out in a restaurant next door, drank heavily, and insulted us every time we walked by. Before long they demanded "protection money" and then kept raising the amount we had to pay. Finally they insisted upon a huge sum and threatened to kill us by a certain date if we didn't comply.

It wasn't that different from a classic Mafia shakedown, but I'm convinced anti-Semitism played a role as well. No doubt the thugs targeted us because they assumed that as Jews we had unlimited wealth, a common stereotype in the Polish mind. And, based on the unchecked wave of Jew-hatred across the country, they knew the police would refuse to protect us. We must have seemed to them like fair game.

We were all in agreement about how to respond to the extortion: flee to the West. That had been our plan all along, and the death threat simply accelerated the process. There was no point in putting our lives on the line to defend our foothold in Szczecin, no matter how lucrative it might be. So my father and husband bribed a Red Army man to drive us to Berlin, a hundred and twenty kilometers south, in a military truck covered by a tarpaulin. This was a well worn, if highly dangerous, route for the smuggling of human cargo, and several thousand Jews would get out of Poland via Szczecin in 1945. In the middle of a freezing night we left our home and store carrying only a few suitcases. But we also took a pile of cash worth about $3,000, a decent annual salary even in western countries at that time, which we had been able to save in just three months in Szczecin.

That money was much needed as we made our way first to the Soviet sector of Berlin and then to the American side. The former capital of the Reich lay in rubble when we arrived, only half a year after the war's end. And even though the famous wall would not be erected for another decade and a half, it was still risky to cross the border. After spending a night in the Soviet zone in the home of someone my father knew, we hired a guide to lead us through a gap between two damaged and deserted buildings. There, under the cover of darkness, we made our run to freedom.

Once in the American sector we were welcomed by U.S. soldiers. It was the first time I'd seen Americans, and I was startled by a black GI. It wasn't the color of his skin that surprised me, for I'd read about Africans in school, but rather his constant chewing. What is he eating? I wondered, and why doesn't he either swallow it or spit it out? At the time, chewing gum was completely unknown in Eastern Europe. I guess I had a lot to learn about everyday American life.

The soldiers quickly took us to UNRRA (the United Nations Relief and Rehabilitation Agency), which had set up an office in Berlin only a month or two earlier, and we were registered as refugees. There we learned about displaced persons (DP) camps in the American zone of occupation, one near Frankfurt am Main and the other near Munich, where we could stay before emigrating from Europe. Without much thought we chose Frankfurt and were informed that a small military bus would soon be dispatched to take us there. Our goal of starting new lives in Palestine or the West finally seemed within reach.

Unfortunately, I was in no condition to rejoice. I had started to feel abdominal pain on the trip south from Szczecin, and now my undergarments were stained with blood. Mim had insisted

I see a doctor once we arrived in East Berlin, and he told me I was several months pregnant and needed bed-rest. I was astonished by the news. In Szczecin, I hadn't menstruated, but I didn't understand the significance of that. And in any case I had not been on a regular cycle in the past.

Of course I yearned to have children. That was the best response to my immense loss, but I didn't want to be pregnant while we were still in Poland and certainly not while we were in flight. What was I to do now? Remaining in bed was impossible—I'd learned of my condition the night before we were all supposed to enter the American zone and we had no official authorization to be on the Soviet side. As Polish nationals and Jews we could be suspected of anything and arrested at any moment. (Indeed, a month later, the Soviets rounded up as many Jewish refugees as they could find in East Berlin and forcibly brought them to a camp in East Germany.) We weren't even sure that the American side of the border would remain open indefinitely. In fact, it would soon be closed to "infiltrees," as people like us were called. So we continued the arduous journey and did not even pause in West Berlin, thinking, quite rightly as it turned out, that any delay could cause us to miss this golden opportunity. With the rest of my family I boarded the U.S. Army minibus headed for Frankfurt.

By now I was not merely staining—blood was running freely down my thighs. Fortunately I was wearing a cape, which covered the lower part of my body, but the pain and worry grew with every passing hour.

After an all-night trip in wintry weather with long stops at several checkpoints, we were dropped off in a quaint suburb called Hoechst on the southwestern edge of Frankfurt. To this day, I can't figure out why the driver wouldn't or couldn't go all the way to the DP camp; it would have taken him perhaps another half-hour. Instead, we were forced to make the final leg of the journey on our own with great difficulty.

We arrived in Hoechst on a Sunday morning and saw no sign of life. The streets were torn up and deserted. No trolleys, trains, or taxis were running. Finally, we glimpsed a German carrying some items on a little handcart. We paid him to load up our luggage and pull it to the DP camp while we walked alongside—a twelve-kilometer trek in the cold. My husband and father carried me part of the way. I was close to fainting from the loss of blood but if we could reach the Americans, we all thought, medical help would be available.

The large Zeilsheim DP camp was still under construction in late 1945, and the barracks we were assigned were drab and dirty, but at least I could lie down for an hour or two. Isaak, meanwhile, went to the main office and explained that I needed emergency care. By late that day I was transferred to a hospital in a neighborhood near the center of Frankfurt, ironically named Sachsenhausen, although not the site of the infamous concentration camp, which was located near Berlin.

I was the only Jewish patient in the ward of eight women, and of course all the doctors and nurses were German too. We had been on German soil for a few days by then, but being away from the American authorities, in a German hospital under the care of the same people who had served the Reich, made me distraught. Merely hearing them speak their language gave me chills. My bad reaction to the anesthetic they gave me only added to my agitation.

The medical staff stopped the bleeding but otherwise seemed callous to my plight. I couldn't tell if this was their normal demeanor or if they were balking at having to treat a Jew, and an East European refugee at that. One doctor came in and stated the pregnancy test proved negative—the rabbit didn't die, he told me. Therefore my problem could very well be uterine cancer. With that, Mim flew into a rage and began cursing him in Yiddish. She grabbed him by the collar. "This girl did not survive Hitler in order to die here!" she shouted.

Later another dour man in a white coat entered and reported that I had, indeed, been pregnant. He then held up a jar with a five-month-old male fetus in it and said it was mine. If that weren't enough, he told me I would never survive another pregnancy and should forget about ever having children. Now I lost any self-control I had left. Fate had robbed me of my mother and brothers and now of any offspring. The person standing nearest to my bed was a nurse and I started kicking her in the stomach and leg as hard as I could. They had to tie me down to restrain me.

I stayed in that hospital a little longer to regain my strength after the miscarriage and then rejoined my family in Zeilsheim. In the few weeks I'd been away, a lot had changed. We now occupied the ground floor of a comfortable two-family cottage, and I convalesced on a bed of my own. Food was available, and visitors began to come over. Father, who had bought a *tallis* on one of his trips to Lodz but never wore it in Chelm or Szczecin, once again began to wrap himself in it daily and recite his morning prayers. For the first time since 1939 we regularly celebrated Shabbes and the other Jewish holidays. Above all, we were part of a Jewish community once more. The DP camps were the only vibrant ones left in Europe.

This would be our "preparatory school" for life in a free country, and it enabled us to find purpose and meaning again. I would even get the chance to prove those German doctors wrong. But I could not imagine then that we would remain displaced persons for well over three years.

8 | LIBERATED, NOT YET FREE

THE FIVE THOUSAND JEWS OF Zeilsheim were frustrated by having to wait so long in a kind of holding pen on German soil. We had just endured the worst trauma imaginable, and almost every one of us wanted to get to the next stage in life, whether it was in Palestine, in America, or somewhere else.

Luckily, our DP camp was one of the best, providing us with decent food and housing, religious and educational activities, and above all physical safety, the first step toward reentering the civilized world. In Zeilsheim we had a synagogue and a yeshiva, a newspaper and sports clubs. I even remember picking up a nice dress from a seamstress in the camp, getting my hair done, and going to the opera in nearby Wiesbaden. Only a few months earlier, I'd been terrorized by anti-Semitic Polish thugs, and only a few years before that, I'd subsisted in a wintry forest like a hunted animal.

It's true that the staples we received from UNRRA, which

included a lot of powdered milk and eggs, weren't very tempting. But like the other DPs, we weren't limited to that fare because we were also issued ample amounts of coffee, chocolate, and cigarettes, items that could easily be sold or traded on the black market for fresh meat and vegetables—and much more. The four of us shared a nice two-bedroom unit, and I can still see Mim stirring big pots of chicken, turkey, duck, or goose, the aroma filling the house. And the birds were kosher, ritually slaughtered by a *shochet* right there in the camp.

Once I recovered from my miscarriage, I enrolled in Modern Hebrew, one of the many courses offered at Zeilsheim, since I thought we'd probably make *aliyah*. My father, meanwhile, tutored youngsters in Talmud and prepared a few for bar mitzvah; I hadn't seen him so content since before the war. Because so few of his age had survived, he was treasured by the younger generation and called simply *Shveyer*, father-in-law. He often served as a peacemaker and one time heroically stepped in to prevent some vengeful Jews from administering a severe beating to a Ukrainian who'd wandered into the Jewish section of the camp.

But Isaak thrived the most. The former Betar leader now got deeply enmeshed in Zionist politics and spent countless hours planning events, raising funds, and helping Jews get to Palestine. Every week he went to meetings, some of them secret, not only in Zeilsheim but throughout the entire American zone. His hand seemed to be in everything.

The plight of hundreds of thousands of stateless Holocaust survivors constituted a full-scale humanitarian crisis, and many sympathetic world leaders visited Zeilsheim, one of the largest DP camps. It was the first one David Ben-Gurion saw when he toured postwar Europe in 1945, and the following year Eleanor Roosevelt arrived. She was mobbed by adoring survivors and

Eleanor Roosevelt at the Zeilsheim DP camp in 1946. Isaak is in the first row on the right.

escorted by U.S. military officers, camp officials—and Isaak! With an air of authority as a member of the official greeting committee he strode through the camp alongside her as press photographers snapped pictures. I looked down on the scene from my friend's apartment and still remember the former first lady's fox collar, outlandish hat, and squeaky voice. Most of all I was proud of my husband and the leadership he showed. Later, he and my father were instrumental in erecting a monument in Zeilsheim to the victims of the Shoah.

Jewish visitors from other DP camps, where the living conditions were often substandard, were impressed by our good fortune. Among them were my stepmother's brother, Yoinah Zuckerman, his wife, and their two daughters, all of whom had passed as Aryans during the war. (Tragically, a third daughter had been caught and killed.) My husband and father pulled some strings and helped get the Zuckermans transferred to Zeilsheim from an overcrowded camp in West Berlin. Later, Isaak and Tateh helped bring in two other families who had been business partners of the Zuckermans in Lodz immediately after the war, first the Drukiers and then the Gertels, a harder task because they were not relatives.

Yoinah Zuckerman, an accomplished *chazzan*, or cantor, quickly began leading services in the camp and stirred us all with his melodious voice. Along with Tateh, who worked as sort of a *melamed*, and Isaak, who was devoted to Zionism and learned in Talmud, too, we were considered a model Jewish family. Other DPs dubbed us "Chasidim" to indicate our fervor. Maybe this was why Isaak and I were chosen so often, sometimes by couples we barely knew, to lead them down the aisle to the *chuppah*. Isaak

With Isaak on the right and a friend from Luboml on the left.

wore a natty hat for those occasions, and I donned my best dress. We stood in for their murdered parents, and few moments in my life have meant more to me.

There were weddings almost every week at Zeilsheim as young survivors sought to make new lives for themselves. Early on, these were simple affairs like my own nuptials in Chelm, and at the last minute I would often have to scrounge a piece of cloth with which to veil the bride. The chuppah might be an army blanket with a blue Star of David sewn into it; the tables could be covered with bed sheets. But there were some big banquets, too, held in the spacious social hall we called Café Amcha, Hebrew for café of the folk. At one such wedding, it seemed that the whole camp was in attendance. Long counters were laden with food and liquor, and because you could get almost anything in exchange for the right commodities, the groom brought in jazz musicians and palm trees, creating a little tropical paradise in the heart of Germany.

Given all of these marriages, it was hardly surprising that Zeilsheim was soon filled with pregnant women and, by mid-1946, newborn babies. Indeed, the DP camps had one of the highest birth rates in the world. I also got pregnant again as quickly as I could. Nothing was more important than to bring forth a new life, a namesake for my dear Mameh. I hoped for a girl even though I knew Isaak desperately wanted a boy.

Maybe it was irresponsible to have had a child at that point. The doctors were probably right that I'd be putting my life at risk. Not only was my body frail, but my mind was still in turmoil from everything that had happened to us in this disastrous decade. Besides, we didn't know where we'd be heading once we left the camp or how we'd make a living. Yet none of that mattered. All I cared about was starting a new generation of my family.

It was a difficult pregnancy, as I knew it would be. This time I

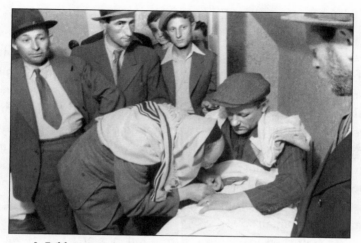

In Zeilsheim my father was sometimes given the high honor of being the sandek, *the man who holds the eight-day-old boy during circumcision.*

was treated by a gynecologist in Hoechst, another unfeeling German physician, whom I never trusted. Late in my term I found out that he had been an SS doctor. Horrified, I never went back to him again. Instead, I put myself in the hands of a prominent professor of OB/GYN at the University of Frankfurt, who, like almost every other German worker in those years of deprivation, charged fees that seemed ridiculously low to us. But while my medical care was excellent and affordable, my condition was not good at all. Under doctor's orders, I had to lie flat on my back at home for five months.

From my bed in our cottage I could see that Isaak and Tateh were involved in a lot more than selling or bartering surplus goods to needy Germans. That kind of petty illegal dealing was sometimes called the "gray market," and almost all DPs participated in it. Usually they took articles they'd gotten from UNRAA or the JDC, or bought from American servicemen, and exchange them for cash, fresh produce, or even a watch or camera.

My husband and father and a few close friends, though, were in the black market and conducted a much more elaborate business. They rarely dealt with Germans or even GIs, but rather with other Jews, many of them from outside Zeilsheim, who in their illicit trade had acquired items containing gold and silver—not only jewelry, but also coffee and tea sets, serving dishes, and even mesh handbags. Tateh paced around our little cottage with tiny bottles of chemicals to determine the quality of the shiny surfaces, bought most of these articles for cash, and then took them to a factory where they were melted down for their precious metals. People also brought us gold grains or powder, which he weighed on a small scale.

We trafficked in diamonds, too, but not often. That was a much more complicated field, and without any expertise in gems, father knew he could easily be cheated. However, he and Isaak became quite knowledgeable about objects of gold and silver. Once my husband took the big risk of traveling to Berlin to sell some of those valuables to the Soviet mission there. The Russians were known to pay high prices for almost anything.

Lucrative though it was, the business we did in precious metals was just a sideline. Even more income was generated from trading currency—Reichmarks, military scrip, gold coins, and dollars—all of which gyrated wildly in the open-air exchange known as the *Boerse*, on Pfaffenwiese Street, which ran right through the camp. My husband had a knack for timing the market, and he often reaped a windfall.

He and Tateh also made handsome commissions as money-changers working at home. Jewish refugees from as far away as Belgium would show up with foreign currency, sometimes carrying a whole suitcase of it, sometimes concealing a roll of money in a bodily orifice, and they usually needed dollars or gold in exchange. Under a special light, Isaak searched for imperfections in each bill. If genuine but merely punctured, he'd accept it and later, using egg white as glue, carefully fill the holes with tiny bits of one-dollar bills before passing it on.

Our house was literally awash with all kinds of cash, and my job was counting and sorting it even while I lay in bed. Few people have ever seen five- and ten-thousand-dollar bills, but I did.

All of this money—belonging to my family, to our black market partners, and to other DPs who'd entrusted their gains to us "Chasidim" for safekeeping—needed a more secure spot than our small domicile under the noses of the military police. So we opened bank accounts in Switzerland and deposited the funds there. Only a few years later these funds would be transferred across the Atlantic and enable our friends and us to go into legitimate businesses in America.

A person who helped my family prosper in many ways in Germany was the young, gentlemanly U.S. Army chaplain, Rabbi Nathan Baruch. He undoubtedly received something from Isaak for his efforts, but he didn't use it for personal gain. A recent biography of him by the authoritative historian Alex Grobman confirms what I knew all along: Baruch's only goal was to save Jewish souls, and his participation in the black market served that end alone. He was one of a handful of dedicated American clergy and social workers in postwar Germany whose aggressive efforts to aid the DPs sometimes put him at odds with the US Army, UNRRA, and even the American Jewish Joint Distribution Committee.

He had emigrated as a child with his family from Poland to the Lower East Side, grew up strictly Orthodox, and was ordained before he was twenty. Appalled at the reports of genocide coming out of Europe, he took part in the famous march on the White House of four hundred Orthodox rabbis in October 1943, demanding American intervention.

By September 1946, at the age of twenty-two, he was in Germany with the mission of serving religious DPs in particular. He came with the backing of the Vaad Hatzalah, or Rescue Committee, an American Orthodox group that during the war had obtained special visas for hundreds of rabbis and yeshiva students trapped in the Nazi net. But of course millions of traditional Jews could not get out and perished. The surviving remnant now needed kosher food and Jewish schools, Talmuds and prayer books, and safe havens in Palestine or the West.

In trying to provide all this, the rabbi worked tirelessly for more than two years. But there were many obstacles in his path. The Vaad was under-funded and understaffed, the US Army sometimes anti-Semitic, and the non-governmental organizations overly bureaucratic. So he had no choice but to bend or break the rules, and unfortunately this led to his being removed from his post and sent back to the States in November 1948.

But until then he accomplished an enormous amount. At one point Baruch got his hands on a big supply of whiskey, cigarettes, and coffee and bartered it for paper, ink, and binding materials, with which he printed almost a quarter of a million religious books and pamphlets, distributed to the DPs and other Jews. The American military would later take credit for the "Army Talmud," but in reality the rabbi had to circumvent the authorities in order to publish it.

Although based in Munich, Baruch visited camps throughout the American zone and first came to Zeilsheim for Rosh Hashanah of 1946. I was bedridden and not present when he met Isaak, but I knew they respected one another as activists during this critical time in Jewish history. While Baruch tried to rekindle Torah-true Judaism, Isaak used some of the considerable resources and connections he'd built up through the black market to help Menachem Begin's right-wing Irgun smuggle both illegal immigrants and weapons into Palestine. In 1947, Isaak embarked on an intensive fundraising campaign intended to acquire a ship near Marseilles and load it with fighters, guns, and ammunition. He never uttered the name of the vessel, but it must have been the famous *Altalena*.

We were affluent enough by then to own a late-model Opel and employ a driver. Isaak would be taken around the camp, swoop down on DPs he knew had done well in the black market, and invite them into the back seat for a little chat. He literally put the arm on them until they agreed to make a meaningful donation to support the wide-ranging activities of the Irgun. As for the *Altalena*, it sailed for Tel Aviv in the middle of the War of Independence, but as it neared the coast it was blown up by the Haganah on Ben-Gurion's orders; he feared that Begin might use the arsenal to stage a *coup d'etat*. That was the end of that right-wing militia, but Isaak's passion for a muscular Zionism would never wane.

During those wild years in Zeilsheim, Isaak's audacity sometimes brought him to the brink of disaster. Particularly perilous was big-time cigarette smuggling, a racket largely controlled by gangsters because the profits were astronomical. Cartons could be bought by an American serviceman in the PX for only seventy cents apiece and then sold on the street to the addicted German public for over $100. So truckloads of cigarettes, diverted from trains or warehouses, were valuable indeed, and we agreed to go into partnership on one of these deals. But our accomplices, tough Jews dressed in black leather coats and wearing long sideburns, did not inspire a lot of trust. A character named Mottel was their leader, and even though the job was pulled off successfully he became enraged because he'd sent his share to a Swiss bank through Isaak's channels and somehow the deposit was posted late. Barging into our place, Mottel grabbed Isaak by the throat and almost strangled him. After that we never had anything to do with him or the cigarette business again.

I had a close call of my own in late 1946. Upstairs lived a family of three sisters, and the boyfriend of one of them was highly active in the black market. When he went out, he'd carry his money in a teakettle or put it in the inner tube of a tire he rolled along the street, which I suppose, raised the suspicions of the MPs. One day, they raided the apartment, hauled off the young man, and brought the three girls into our house to be strip-searched by a female MP.

I was the only one at home, in bed, seven months pregnant, and mortified. Was she going to search me next in the same way? In plain sight on the credenza was a brown suitcase filled with cash. Would the MPs open it and then jail us all?

Nothing of the sort happened. The three sisters were released, the Americans left the premises without searching our place, and the lid of that incriminating suitcase remained closed. Evidently, we were not targets of the investigation.

Still, the home invasion left me deeply shaken and I could almost feel the fetus turn around in my womb. In any case, the doctor soon told me I would need a breech delivery; the baby would have to come out feet first, increasing the risk to the newborn and to me. A further complication in my pregnancy was the last thing I wanted to hear.

But that was before I switched to the medical school professor in Frankfurt. He was eventually able to manipulate the position of the baby in my abdomen so I could avoid the breech birth. Even so, the delivery was a harrowing ordeal, an induced labor of seventy-two hours, while I lay under the glaring lights of the operating room surrounded by a whole staff of medical personnel. At one point, when I told the professor I couldn't push anymore, he angrily began to walk away. Only my promise to keep trying got him to return.

Finally, on February 11, 1947, I gave birth—to a beautiful, healthy eight-pound girl—and Bella Pearl Orbuch's blue eyes were open from the first moments she came into the world. Her middle name was that of Isaak's mother, another grandmother she could never know.

I was utterly exhausted, but with tears running down my face, I could hardly contain my joy. The name Bella would be heard in my household again. I'd not only survived the war and overcome illness and despair, but against all odds, I'd made the ultimate investment in the future.

As soon as I came home from the hospital, we hired a nanny, another German girl who would have been happy to work for just the food we gave her. Yet we had trouble finding baby clothes

Soon after Bella's birth.

and shoes, and even diapers, none of which were available in the local stores at any price. Mim resorted to cutting up bed sheets to use as diapers. But then Isaak wrote to Benny Sheingarten, a distant cousin he had in the States, and before long a steady flow of packages arrived with everything Bella needed.

Usually, though, Isaak was so absorbed in the black market, Zionist activities, and camp politics, I wondered if he even knew he had a child. It was different for my father, however, who was cheered to no end by Bella's birth. He proudly carried her on his high shoulders around the entire camp. Tateh and I had endured the darkest hours together, and he considered becoming a *zaydeh* nothing short of miraculous.

Although we were now responsible for a newborn, we didn't cut back on "business," and sometimes I'd look up to find Bella playing in a pile of money. In fact, she even became our cover: Whenever we got wind that the authorities were on the prowl, Mim would take Bella out in the baby carriage after we laid stacks of bills under its little mattress. Fortunately, none of the MPs suspected anything, even though our baby was riding noticeably higher than the others.

Another hiding place was the space between the double doors of our stove. We'd open one side, insert a lot of cash, and then screw it shut—a good strongbox, but you had to remember not to cook something while the money was still in there. We told the nanny never to light the oven without our permission, and when we needed to get into the makeshift vault we'd concoct some errand to get her out of the house.

This was the strange life we led until we left for the States in February 1949, around the time of Bella's second birthday. About a half-year earlier we had to transfer to the nearby Lampertheim camp, because Zeilsheim was being closed. But even there we had a nice house and good friends, and were able to bring along our

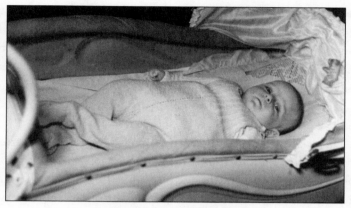

Bella "riding high" around Zeilsheim.

nanny and driver. There was no change in our business routine.

We never felt any moral qualms about our participation in the black market, which enabled us to enjoy some creature comforts while in the DP camps and set something aside for later. What else were we supposed to do? Sit patiently in the land of the killers and play by the rules while the great powers dithered in finding us a home? The Kremlin abided murderous anti-Semites in their satellite countries, and until 1948 Washington held the immigration quotas from Eastern Europe abysmally low while Whitehall kept the gates to Palestine closed.

So we used the time in the camps to our benefit. Due to Nazism I had lost nearly everything, and material goods were the least of it. Now it seemed like the smallest measure of justice to trade a box of chocolates for a well-tailored suit of clothes, or a few cartons of cigarettes for some gold jewelry. It was like reparations before there were reparations. The authorities claimed that the black market was hurting the emerging post-war German economy; somehow that argument failed to move me.

Yes, we were more than small-time operators; we ran a brisk

clearinghouse for the DP community and profited from it. But at the same time we provided a valuable service to many a Jewish refugee and supported some vital causes. Beyond all the money raised for the Irgun, and the contributions Baruch must have received for his important work, we gladly dipped into our stash to aid illegal immigrants on their way to Palestine, some of whom even lacked decent clothes.

One wayfarer we helped was Menachem Ehrlich, a friend of my brother Meir. But as a principled socialist Zionist, Menachem refused our offer to set him up for awhile in the black market. Instead, he went directly to Palestine and worked as a typesetter.

By the end of our time in Germany we were pulling in about $1,000 a day. Some Jews who did well financially opted to stay permanently, buying real estate and raising their children in Frankfurt or Munich. I needn't say this never crossed our minds. The only question for us was whether to go to Palestine or America, and the sooner the better—regardless of what we'd be giving up financially.

Making aliyah was of course Isaak's first choice, the fulfillment of his boyhood dreams. He spoke Hebrew well and had friends in Tel Aviv, but most of all he believed in the return of the Jewish people to its ancient homeland. Yet I fought him on this tremendous decision in our lives. I too was a fervent Zionist—I still am today—but I simply couldn't live through another war, and all the reports from the Middle East pointed to a long, violent struggle ahead. Many prospective immigrants didn't even make it to the Holy Land but were stopped at sea by the Royal Navy and interned behind barbed wire in Cyprus. With the welfare of my baby uppermost in my mind, I begged Isaak to consider the States. Tateh and Mim agreed with me.

I wasn't sure I could prevail against such a determined man, but after a lot of arguing we finally agreed on a compromise: We'd apply to both countries and immigrate to whichever accepted us first. As it turned out, neither option was legally open to us until May 1948, when Israel declared its independence, struck down Britain's notorious White Paper, and welcomed Jews from all over the world.

But that spring and summer saw the fiercest fighting of the war and, before it calmed down, the American consulate in Frankfurt notified us that our visas had come through. The Zuckermans preceded us—Yoinah had received a formal invitation to be a cantor at a *shul* in Williamsburg, Brooklyn—and once he settled in the States he sent an affidavit to the immigration authorities on our behalf. Isaak gave in and to my relief rarely voiced any regrets about it in all the years to come.

I didn't know any English beyond what I'd overheard from American officials in the DP camps, but we had a few months to prepare for the voyage, so I began studying in earnest. A German tutor came to our house three times a week, not surprisingly for a minimal fee. Amidst the hurly-burly of the black market and the distractions of my infant, I learned grammar and vocabulary, though as I'd find out later in New York, the British English I was taught would be of limited use. Still, I had mastered the basics of the language before we left, and I was the only one in my family to have done so.

With a lot of emotion, we parted from our little staff. The nanny was so attached to our family that she wanted to join us in America, but that was not possible. To our chauffeur, a likeable Jewish youth named David, we left the Opel in gratitude for his reliable service.

But it wouldn't be as easy to get out of Germany as we'd thought. First we had to go through a battery of medical tests at the American army base at Butzbach, near Frankfurt. X-rays revealed calcification in my lungs, and I was required to return the next day for a further examination. For twenty-four hours I feared that we wouldn't be able to go, but thankfully my condition was not deemed serious enough to deny me entry. Greatly relieved, we all set off by rail for the emigration center at Bremen, a few hundred kilometers north.

By now, however, Bella had taken sick and was running a very high fever. Again I worried we'd be held back and possibly never regain our places in the immigration queue. But the overheated train compartment had a good effect on my toddler; she seemed to "sweat out" her illness and was fine the next morning when we were processed in Bremen and then transferred by bus to the port of Bremerhaven on the North Sea.

Everything will be all right as soon as we leave this accursed

My westward journey, 1944-49.

Our ship to America, the Marine Jumper.

country and continent, I thought. But we sailed on the *Marine Jumper*, a rusty, battered troop ship converted to passenger use, and the two-week-long midwinter crossing was a nightmare from the moment we passed through the English Channel. The boat was tossed around by huge storms and swells, and it felt like the captain never got out of the path of a hurricane.

Men were berthed separately from women, so I was in a cabin with Mim and Bella, and we could hardly keep the baby's crib from sliding around and banging into the walls. At one point my family sat down with other passengers in the ship's dining room, at tables set with fine linen and china—and suddenly everything crashed to the floor. Not that we had much appetite: Except for my father we were all retching with seasickness. We consumed mainly water and tea, brought to us by Tateh, and we gave Bella a lot of tea as well. Isaak suffered the most and never went into his cabin; he stayed on deck, vomiting over the side, day and night, while being splashed with waves of seawater. When we finally reached New York he was such a mess that I had to clean him up from head to toe. I wanted us to look presentable for our first encounter with the New World, so I ironed his rumpled clothes, but I never found out what happened to his shoelaces.

It was exhilarating to see the Statue of Liberty, even though nausea marred the experience. I don't know why we didn't choose a proper ocean liner like the *Queen Mary*—or just fly, since trans-Atlantic flights were already in operation. We certainly could have afforded options other than the *Marine Jumper*. But none of us imagined how rough a journey it would be.

We all felt better once we came ashore and were greeted by Mim's brother, Yoinah, and his wife, Yitka. We put our luggage into two big, old-fashioned taxis and headed from Lower Manhattan over the bridge to Brooklyn. I was stunned by the size of the skyscrapers and the city itself—like nothing I'd ever seen. Once we got to Williamsburg, though, things looked awfully drab. The Zuckermans' apartment was warm and comfortable, and Yitka was a great cook, which was especially welcome after having eaten so little on our long journey. But all I saw out the window were other brick apartment houses. Worse, the streets were littered with garbage and old newspapers. Could all of America be so filthy? There *was* one good thing about Germany, I realized—the clean streets.

I was also disappointed that we'd brought exactly the wrong German goods to America. We could have transported Rosenthal china or Meissen porcelain but Isaak was afraid of damage in transit. Instead, we acted upon Yoinah's suggestion of bringing a steamer trunk of *gatkes*—yes, underwear—which he said was in short supply in the United States and would fetch a high price. We ended up donating most of it to charity.

It was disheartening, too, not being able to decipher the language. It might have been different had we immigrated to a place where they spoke the King's English. The Brooklyn dialect, though, was virtually unintelligible. Something like "Trow it out da windeh," made no sense to me whatsoever.

In the two months we stayed with the Zuckermans, I saw

that I had a lot to learn. But I was only twenty-three years old and eager to begin. Although we'd experienced some minor mishaps, I felt I'd steered my family in the right direction. But right or wrong, we'd made our choice and committed ourselves to America. I was determined to make the most of it.

9 | PROMISED LAND

THINGS WOULD IMPROVE, I THOUGHT, once we were no longer guests in someone else's home, but it wasn't easy to find a place we could call our own. We had to compete with the many returning American servicemen, most starting new families, and the search for appropriate housing was a monumental task. As the weeks dragged on at the Zuckermans, I felt so desperate I even considered a shabby apartment on a crime-ridden stretch of Pitkin Avenue, next to a stable.

Then Isaak and my father, getting a little fretful themselves, came up with a completely different plan: The family would move to a chicken farm. It may sound peculiar, but raising poultry was then the vocation of thousands of East European Jewish refugees on both the East and the West Coasts. It was hard work, seven days a week, but you could get started quickly and make money by selling the eggs or the birds.

In our region the hub of the industry was Vineland, New Jersey, about a hundred miles southeast of New York City. Without discussing it much with Mim or me, Isaak and Tateh traveled there by bus one Sunday, winding their way through back country roads, and returned at night with the news that we were going to be chicken ranchers. I wasn't thrilled with the idea, but before I could utter a word, it was clear they themselves had doubts about settling in a rural area. "What did we just do?" they asked one another, wallowing in buyer's remorse. "With whom am I going to talk, with whom am I going to *daven*—the chickens?" wailed my father. First thing the next morning, Isaak went to the bank and canceled his $500 deposit.

Finally, in early spring, Isaak and my father landed something far better. They bought a sturdy prewar house in the middle-class section of Bensonhurst, a neighborhood predominantly of Southern Italians and East European Jews. It was close to a *shtiebel* where the men could daven, and not too far from the shore, where Bella could play. Originally, it was an ample single-family home, but it had been converted into two separate residences. The five of us moved into the owners' downstairs quarters. Mim and I shared the housework; she shopped and cooked, and I cleaned, beginning a pattern of teamwork that would last for decades. We continued to keep the second floor as a rental unit, which helped pay the mortgage. Only months earlier we had come off the boat; now we were homeowners and landlords.

Other *grineh,* Yiddish for "greenhorns," felt so much pressure to make it in America they attempted to create a false impression. I had some distant relatives who had been in the States for years and worked hard running a small business. Just before we moved to Bensonhurst, they had us over to their home for dinner, and everything seemed rather plain except for their sparkling set of dishes. I found out later they'd been bought from Macy's just for the occasion and returned the following day.

In front of our home in Bensonhurst, Brooklyn. From left, Wolf,
Isaak, Bella, me, and my stepmother, Chava, whom I called Mim.

Other immigrants wanted to be sure we knew the hardships they'd suffered earlier in the century, and how easy we had it by comparison. That's what Isaak, Tateh, and I encountered at the Luboml *landsmanshaft*, the fraternal society of people from my hometown living in the New York area. I was nicely dressed in a navy blue coat, accessorized with a burgundy hat and handbag. Soon after we entered, a group of old ladies noticed us from across the room, and one of them pointed at me and in earshot of everyone declared: "So this is the grineh! When *we* came to America we had to carry the coal and seltzer bottles up to the fifth floor."

What was the point? I wondered. She knew nothing about my family or me and probably couldn't imagine that we'd endured a lot worse than living in a tenement. I didn't return to the landsmanshaft for many years.

I noticed early on that many of those who had immigrated decades earlier didn't speak English well. To me, the language was the entryway to becoming an American, and I resolved to become proficient in it. Bella would soon be starting school, and I didn't want to embarrass her or myself by not being able to speak correctly or write a proper note to her teachers. We spoke a lot of Yiddish at home—I could hardly expect Tateh and Mim, now in their late fifties, to become fluent in a new tongue overnight—but I tried to train my ear to English by listening to the radio as much as possible. I also studied the language in night school, and I read all the time, just as I had as a schoolgirl in Luboml.

English also came quickly to Isaak, who, like me, had learned many languages as a youth: Polish, Ukrainian, Russian, Yiddish, German, and Hebrew. His knack for English was a good thing, too, because he had to find a way to make a living. True, we had some capital, but none of us had a profession, and our contacts were limited almost exclusively to other grineh.

Luckily, we got some good advice from our Americanized cousins. Joe Orbuch, who had immigrated decades earlier, coincidentally owned a small hotel in partnership with a relative of mine, Louis Shames. They both suggested we buy and operate a rooming house. Before long, one came on the market in Manhattan, the La Plata on 104th Street between Amsterdam and Columbus Avenues, a property with dozens of small units, most of them with kitchenettes.

It could be acquired for a down payment of only $15,000 in cash, but the aging, eight-story building entailed a great deal of risk. Without an established line of credit, and not yet a citizen, Isaak didn't even try for a commercial mortgage from a bank. He had to rely on private lenders in our refugee community—and paid a very high interest rate. Beyond that, the Upper West Side was not a choice neighborhood (it would not become one for decades) and the La Plata was located in one of its roughest pockets. Tenants rented rooms by the week or month, which naturally drew a low-income clientele including a lot of young, single transients. But Isaak, with his characteristic courage and acumen, looked beyond these problems and saw the potential.

My father was a partner and operated the elevator; it was the old-fashioned kind that had to be stopped manually with a big lever at just the moment it came even with the floor. And Yoinah Zuckerman was brought into the deal as well to be the front man, or desk clerk. Having immigrated a couple of years before us, Yoinah's English was already passable, though it would have been even better had he spoken Spanish, too. We laughed at his stories of some Puerto Ricans who seemed to know even less English than we did; a few of them asked for rooms with a chicken when they meant kitchen. Yoinah, whose cantorial work brought in very little money, didn't have the funds to buy into the partnership, so we laid it out for him, and were paid back in a short time.

Isaak, the overall troubleshooter, got up early, put on a nice suit and tie, and took the subway uptown, where he worked all day to make the La Plata successful. Just cleaning up the dank basement, full of junk and toxic residue, was a formidable task, and he did most of it himself with little more than rubber gloves and an apron. He drummed up business, supervised the repairmen, and "negotiated" with the city inspectors. He made sure the rooming house was secure, clean, and quiet. Once in a while he had to deal with deadbeats: if they were deeply in arrears, he'd lock them out of their rooms until they paid at least something.

In a short time the La Plata generated a healthy stream of revenue, and it emboldened Isaak to purchase a more upscale rooming house in a better part of town on the East Side, on 95th Street near Lexington Avenue. For that venture, Joe Orbuch was his partner and the property's manager. Isaak would make more than half a dozen other lucrative Manhattan real estate investments throughout the rest of the 1950s, moving up from rooming houses to hotels, which he bought in partnership with many former DPs, like the Drukiers, with whom we'd been close in Zeilsheim.

In purchasing the seventeen-story Regent on Broadway and 104th, which had been an architectural gem in the 1920s but was now in decline, he went in with ten partners, including Charles Drukier and Robert Born, whose families would later become major players in the New York hotel industry. Isaak made the Regent his main base of operations, while Tateh and Yoinah took over the management of the La Plata just a couple of blocks away.

Isaak on 104th Street near Broadway in front of the Regent Hotel.

The three of them were also part owners of the smaller Stratford and Aberdeen hotels down on 34th Street near the Empire State Building. Later, Isaak invested with many of the same partners in the stately Wellington Hotel in Midtown.

The insurance man on most of these properties was Nathan Baruch, the army chaplain from Zeilsheim. He was still deeply involved in the yeshiva world, but after his return from Germany he established a thriving insurance business. Many of his best clients were survivors like us whom he had personally helped in the DP camps and who now returned the favor.

Isaak's real estate attorney and two tax accountants were all Yiddish-speaking relatives. He gladly turned his list of professional contacts over to any new immigrant who needed it and dispensed a lot of free advice, too, encouraging many a newcomer to go into the rooming house or hotel business, just as he had been advised several years earlier. Having seen several grineh struggle as the owners of laundromats, five-and-dimes, or small eateries, he felt that real estate, with all its uncertainties, was a better path toward financial security.

An early sign of our own prosperity was the big Buick Roadmaster Isaak bought soon after he'd gotten the La Plata humming. He was the first in our circle of friends to own an automobile, but that didn't mean he knew how to operate it. He never took a driving lesson, and I don't remember him passing any test at the Department of Motor Vehicles. I suspect he obtained his license some other way. And it showed: Every time he backed out of our garage was an adventure. In fact, the neighbors would gather on the sidewalk, some shaking their heads and others laughing out loud, as Isaak labored to maneuver the bulky Buick in reverse through the narrow driveway between our house and the one next door.

Any Brooklyn cop wanting to give out more citations could

simply wait for my husband on Stillwell Avenue, where there was a good chance he'd miss the stop sign. After a while, Isaak took to placing a twenty-dollar bill opposite the license in his billfold. Each time he was pulled over, he'd open it and the police officer, if he were on the take, would pocket the twenty. If not, Isaak would receive yet another ticket, but at least he could plausibly deny that he was offering a bribe. When I think back on it now, I'm amazed at how brazen he could be.

Isaak had a lot to be thankful for by the early '50s, but what he wanted most was a son, not only to continue the family name, but even more importantly to be a "Kaddish," as the expression went, because in traditional Jewish circles only males recite the prayer for a dead parent. I wasn't ready to oblige him, though. It took a lot of emotional energy to raise one child, and besides I feared the pregnancy would knock me flat on my back again for many months.

But Isaak persuaded me to have another baby, and I did have a lot of physical discomfort at the outset: I was so nauseous that I couldn't stand the odor of meat cooking and literally had to run from the kitchen. I lost ten pounds in a short time, just the wrong thing for someone pregnant. But after the first trimester I somehow felt a lot better and the delivery, in the summer of 1951 at Maimonides Hospital in Borough Park, was easier than I'd feared. I had a boy, whom we named Paul and to whom we gave the Hebrew names Pesach Zvi for Isaak's father and my Uncle Hershel. What a thrilling moment, to know that I'd made my husband's fondest wish come true. Now we had a complete family, a boy and a girl.

It was customary then for new mothers to spend a lot of time recuperating in the hospital after giving birth. With my track record, the doctors didn't release me for more than a week, so I missed all the festivities, even the bris. But I heard about everything, including a gala celebration called Shalom Zachor, so held in our home on the Friday evening before the circumcision, a special event to welcome the birth of a male, which an ecstatic Isaak wouldn't forego, whether I was there or not.

After Paul's birth, our living quarters got a bit crowded, so we asked the tenants upstairs to leave and turned the unit over to my father and Mim. By 1954, with our business continuing to expand, we moved out of Bensonhurst into a lovely home in a fine neighborhood in Queens—the Crescents of Rego Park. The name refers to five narrow semi-circular streets of good-sized houses on ample lots. We bought the new home after seeing the developer's plans; it was one of only a few two-family homes available in that up-and-coming neighborhood. Bella and Paul each had their own room, and of course the second, identical unit went to Tateh and Mim. As they did in Brooklyn, my parents took in a boarder, less for help in making expenses than to do a good deed by easing a bachelor's loneliness. For many years the divorced brother-in-law of Mim's niece lived with them; we all treated him as a member of the family.

In time, some of our partners in the hotel business, like the Drukiers and Peltzes, moved into the Crescents, and soon most of the other houses, too, were occupied by successful refugees: the Pomerances, the Blaichmans, the Schwartzes, the Kalts, the Kravitzes, the Krakowskis, and many others. Our children were together all the time, the neighbors did anything they could for one another, and it almost felt like the close-knit clan in which I'd been raised. My extended family had been annihilated but Paul and Bella grew up with a lot of aunts, uncles, and cousins nonetheless.

Tateh, now in his sixties and semi-retired, once again carried his tallis and t'fillin to daven in a Chasidic minyan, but instead of Luboml's Stepenyer shil'chl, it was now the Queens shtiebel of

Rabbi Pekarsky. Father soon became president of the little brick prayer house, on a residential street, and donated a new ark, Torah cover, and reader's table. He had a slogan that expressed his benevolent nature: "Give with warm hands," meaning give while you're still alive.

Isaak, meanwhile, was one of the founders of an Orthodox congregation, Young Israel of Forest Hills, which soon erected a substantial new synagogue. Also, he occasionally served as a *bohrer*, or advocate, for individuals seeking redress in a *Din Torah*, the rabbinical court our community used to settle internal disputes. Three rabbis decided each case according to Jewish law, and Isaak's keen reasoning and forceful presentation usually carried the day for his side.

We enrolled Bella and later Paul in the nearby modern Orthodox—and staunchly Zionist—Yeshiva Dov Revel, which had just constructed a new, well-equipped schoolhouse. Paul flourished there, but my daughter was unhappy in the yeshiva because her class had few girls and most of her friends from our neighborhood attended the nearby public school. After the sixth grade we sent her to a public junior high school. Yet overall, I was amazed with how much we could revive of the rich Jewish life we'd enjoyed in Luboml. Seeing my father sitting by the window and reading a passage from a handsome edition of *Pirke Avos*, and knowing he'd discuss it with my son when he came home from school, filled me with a quiet joy.

My own energies were devoted to Zionist activities. I co-founded a branch of Hadassah, the Tel Chai chapter of Rego Park-Forest Hills, made up exclusively of survivors, and became its vice-president for fundraising and education. Part of my work was persuading some of the members to attend events in Manhattan, another world for a lot of grineh. I also needed to do a lot of public speaking, which made me nervous—I still get stage fright in front of large audiences—but as one the best English speakers in our group I was called upon often. I'd practice my speeches in front of Mim, who took a motherly pride in the new role I'd assumed.

The main goal, though, was to make a difference in people's lives. Through Hadassah, my friends and I raised a lot of money for Youth Aliyah, which furthered the ingathering to Israel and the education there of youngsters from Eastern Europe and North Africa. I was also the co-initiator of a local chapter of Akim, which aids disabled children in Israel. In these causes I worked closely with many powerful women. One I've admired immensely over the years is the late Eta Wrobel of Flushing, a sole survivor and former partisan who demonstrated exceptional leadership in countless Jewish organizations. When I learned that in the forest she had once extracted a bullet from her own leg, I wasn't surprised.

There was a function to attend every week, it seemed, and busy though he was at work, Isaak loved to get dressed up at night and accompany me to the Pierre, Plaza, or Waldorf. He not only willingly sent generous checks to many Jewish charities but also helped a good number of people directly, especially survivors in need of lodging.

Addressing a gathering with Eta Wrobel.

Among them were the Warsaw-born musicians Chaim and Sara Fershko, whose story was one of the most tearful, but ultimately uplifting, I'd ever heard. She was a concert violinist and opera singer, he a pianist, and they'd been sent by the Soviet high command to entertain partisans behind enemy lines. They were captured by the Germans, and as punishment their left arms were amputated at the shoulder, without anesthesia. Yet after the war they resumed their careers in New York. Chaim played the piano one-handed, and Sara accompanied him with her soulful voice. They held many recitals and once performed on the *Ed Sullivan Show* (although no mention was made on television about how their bodies had been mutilated). Still, they struggled financially. Isaak housed them and their attendant at the Regent for many years without charge and even bought them a piano.

While the trauma of the war was still with us, we did enjoy a lot of carefree hours in the 1950s, especially in the summers, when we fled to the Catskills to escape the city heat. The first year, I stayed alone with Bella in a hotel, the Loch Shellbrook, which despite its fancy Scottish name, was run by Luboml Jews. I was lonely there because most of the guests were elderly and I had little in common with them. Also, I was sometimes taken aback by the brusque commands they issued to the dining room staff, mostly kids working their way through college or graduate school. Isaak, Tateh, and Mim came up only occasionally on the weekends.

Beginning the next year, we spent every July and August at a bungalow colony, and that was *freylach*, a lively, happy time. Like almost everyone else heading for the Catskills in these pre-Thruway years, my family, including Tateh and Mim, drove up on old Route 17, stopping along the way at the Red Apple for a bagel and lox, a tomato and herring sandwich, or gefilte fish. It marked the halfway point to "the country" or "the mountains"

At the bungalow colony in the Catskills. Isaak and I are in the lower right. My father is at the head of the table holding cards; my stepmother stands behind him. Her brother and sister-in-law, Yoinah and Yitka Zuckerman are in the upper right. Charles Druckier sits between my father and me.

as we referred to our vacation spot near Monticello, New York, which really wasn't that far from the five boroughs nor that high above sea level.

I had many good friends in the bungalow colony, like the Dunietzes, whom I'd known back in Poland, and other families like the Barads, Kaliksteins, Pragers, Shames's, Speismans, Rubens, and Joe and Sarah Orbuch. We were especially close to the Zuckermans and their daughters, Ruth and Sally. We had a day camp for the kids and variety shows for the adults. Each year we gathered our friends together to celebrate our anniversary, and once the gang threw me a big surprise party. I'd left for a few days to finalize my naturalization process in the city, and when I returned, as a newly minted American citizen, Isaak brought me over to the social hall, which we called the casino. It was dark when I opened the door, so I turned on the light and was met by the smiles and cheers of dozens of my friends. They'd decorated the room in red, white, and blue.

Isaak had to work during the summers, but like most of the other breadwinners he came up every weekend. On the way he'd pick up hitchhikers, usually bearded, traditional Jews, and didn't seem to care how many piled into the Roadmaster. He'd buy them all a meal on the way and drop them off at their destinations.

When he finally came to us late Friday afternoon my husband had a ritual. First he slipped into his trunks and took Paul—thrilled to be with his father—for a quick swim in the pool. Invariably it was already closed, but Isaak wouldn't be deterred; he'd get the key to the gate from the proprietor, and the two Orbuch males had the pool to themselves. Afterward, he'd dry off and immediately head for a friendly game of poker with his buddies. After a week's hard work and a long, hot drive, I suppose he needed that kind of relaxation, but all I got was a perfunctory greeting. I complained to him again and again that after we'd been apart for five straight days, I craved his attention, too. But after a while I gave up; I could tell this was one battle I'd never win.

Still, those summers were blissful, and I see now how much we grineh needed to be with our own in order to relax. Among

A wedding anniversary in the Catskills.

The Buick Roadmaster with Paul on the hood.

ourselves we could tell stories and jokes in Yiddish or Polish and not have to worry about the reproach of outsiders.

By the late 1950s, I had more time for myself than ever before. When Bella was ten, we sent her to a sleep-away camp for two full months. I could leave Paul with his grandparents and come into the city to work with an interior decorator and oversee the painting and remodeling of my house.

During the rest of the year, we celebrated Thanksgiving and Passover with Mim's family, the Zuckermans, and threw many big and lively parties besides. Because so few from my father and Mim's generation had survived the war, our friends became their friends, and she and I did so much entertaining together that it became second nature. She'd bake in her apartment upstairs while I prepared the menu, shopped, and set the table. When guests arrived, they had cocktails in the Orbuch home, then went up to the Shainwalds for dinner, then later came downstairs again for dessert.

We loved to go out, too, and our friends used to say about Isaak, "First on the road, last off the dance floor." They were wonderful years, the 1950s, even if the horrible memories of the decade before remained fresh in my mind. I had a marvelous family and a comfortable life; I lived in a free country as a proud Jew.

Little did I know that at age thirty-five my happiness was about to come to a shocking end.

In 1960, Isaak began suffering from neurological problems, and his condition deteriorated for thirty-seven years until he passed away in 1997. In different ways, the malady tortured us both for that entire time.

The first symptoms were so minor and came on so slowly, I barely noticed anything wrong. But concerned friends took me aside and mentioned that he had difficulty putting his arm through his coat sleeve. And I saw that when he walked, his left arm swung normally at his side, but his right arm remained rigid. He continued to putter around in the garage and repair things in the house, but a neighbor observed that Isaak seemed uncharacteristically slow while on a ladder painting the siding.

Like many men of his generation, he rarely discussed the state of his personal health, even with his wife. But this time I insisted he see our family doctor, Julius Stein, a neighbor and a dear friend, whose son, Sidney, and Paul were the best of buddies. Julie, as we called him, had his practice on Fifth Avenue, and Isaak went there alone. He returned with a referral to the head neurologist at Columbia-Presbyterian Hospital.

I came along to this appointment. Isaak drove, and sitting beside him I was only mildly worried. A pill, maybe some physical therapy, there's a good chance it will all be fine, I thought. The truly terrible possibilities I pushed to the furthest margins of my mind.

The neurologist, a tall handsome man, examined him thoroughly, went into another office for a few minutes and then returned with the diagnosis—Parkinson's disease.

This was the worst verdict we could get, and it hit me with the force of a lead pipe. I knew there was no cure—in those days there was not even any medication for it—and that it meant a progressive, degenerative loss of control over one's body. Having discussed this fearsome possibility in some detail with Dr. Julie Stein, Isaak knew even more than I did about the ravaging effects of the disease. He now tried to hold himself together in the examining room but was clearly distraught.

Through my tears I begged the diagnosing physician for an answer to how this could happen to such a vigorous, forty-five-year-old man. I thought of him roughhousing with Paul on the floor, or taking the kids swimming, skating, fishing or horseback riding. He was a bundle of energy, always on the go, at work or at home.

The doctor had no explanation. He told me that Parkinson's usually occurs later in life but that physical fitness is no predictor of the illness. It was not known what caused the chemical changes that scrambled the signals transmitted by the brain. The disease would gradually worsen, he added, but Isaak might be able to delay the worst effects with exercises and massage.

In desperation I asked the neurologist if research was being conducted into Parkinson's Disease. Could the future hold any remedy at all, maybe a miracle drug? He pondered my question for a moment and then took my hand and led me to the window. "Look over there," he said, pointing to a construction pit where a new medical building would be going up. "That will be a center for the study of Parkinson's, and that's the status of our research now—we're laying the foundations." I was hardly encouraged.

Isaak and I drove back home mostly in silence as we each tried to come to grips with the momentous meaning of the past hour. What would happen to his body as the disease ran its terrible course? What would happen to us when he couldn't work anymore? How would our family, friends, and business partners react to him as an invalid? And, like everyone else who's been dealt such a crushing blow, we asked why. Why did this good man have to be afflicted with something so horrible?

It was still early in the afternoon when we entered the house, and the kids weren't yet home from school. Isaak flung himself on Paul's bed and wept. In the fifteen years of our marriage, I'd never known him to shed a tear. "I'd rather die than have you see me in a wheelchair," he moaned.

But in reality he would never give up and neither would I. We were both fighters and no strangers to life's cruelties.

10 | THE NEW ENEMY

AFTER THE DIAGNOSIS WE CLUNG to the belief that the disease would move slowly, that with a rigorous regime of physical therapy many years would elapse before the monster inflicted its worst damage.

But it soon became undeniable that Isaak's body was rapidly losing ground to the invader.

One of the first things to deteriorate was his manual dexterity. Before the illness, his manicured hands could perform the most precise tasks. He once drew up a multiplication table on a little card to help Paul with his homework; the numbers were tiny but so clearly written and neatly arranged they were easily readable. And his penmanship, in Hebrew and English, had been impeccable. But now his handwriting was reduced to a nearly indecipherable scrawl.

Playing draw poker with his friends became another humbling experience. He had had his own style of looking at his cards, squeezing them open ever so slightly to get a peek at the corners. Now he handled his cards awkwardly and was slow and clumsy picking up and discarding them; his right hand sometimes shook uncontrollably. His friends were patient at first but soon they wanted to go on with the game: "Nu, Isaak, do something already." Later, when he couldn't play at all anymore, they'd invite him to the weekly card games just to kibbitz. It was an important part of our social life, the men playing poker in one room, the women playing fourteen-card gin rummy in another, but before long we had to give it up. Isaak was too embarrassed to sit on the sidelines.

Worst of all, though, were the mounting problems at business because Isaak was responsible for the payroll and wasn't up to all the paperwork required. So I got into the habit of going in to work with him a few times a month, and I'd be the one to prepare the pay packets—behind locked doors.

For we both felt it vital that no one learn of Isaak's growing infirmity, least of all his business partners. Our livelihood depended on a network of personal relationships, and if Isaak's associates believed he was incapacitated, they might think twice before including him in any more real estate deals.

While my father, my stepmother, Mim, and the kids saw that something was seriously wrong, I tried to shield even them from the full truth of his condition. I felt especially protective toward my dear father, whom I'd wanted to spare from pain since I was a little girl in Luboml. In the 1960s he suffered from several heart attacks, and I was always anxious about the state of his health; I couldn't bear to add to his worries. So there were many times when I cried, but rarely in front of my family. Of course, our physician and friend, Julie Stein, knew everything, and I also confided in two other neighbors, Breineh and David Kalt, who were in our home often. She had been a former partisan, and her first husband had died of cancer at age forty-two, so we understood each other well. But I did my best to keep almost all of my other close friends in the dark.

In today's America people are very open about the most devastating diseases—their own or a loved one's—but a generation ago, especially in my circle, it was different. That information was kept private, which suited me because I didn't want to be the object of anyone's pity or burden a fellow Holocaust survivor with my problems.

Beyond that, was an overriding sense of shame. Maybe this came from the culture of the shtetl, in which people with disabilities were often stigmatized. Or it went back even further to the lepers in the Bible, cast out by God himself. True, we knew of the compassion that Judaism teaches, that it's a great mitzvah to visit and care for the sick, but we were also aware of the superstition and ignorance surrounding this kind of affliction.

In this period—way before Michael J. Fox, Janet Reno, Morris Udall, and Muhammad Ali gave human faces to Parkinsonism—we feared Isaak would be shunned if people knew he had "the shaking palsy." In fact, one or two of our neighbors seemed to cross the street when they saw him approaching, as if they thought his ungainly stride was contagious. So during the many years when the physical therapist came over, we closed the windows and drew the shades. If anyone rang the bell for Isaak, we said he wasn't home.

At first, the secret physiotherapy was our only chance to hold the illness at bay. Bob Glicken, who led Isaak through an hour-long series of exercises three times a week, became almost like a member of the family. He said, only half-jokingly, that we'd already paid him enough to buy his car, and now he was working toward a down payment on a house. Bob was a good man and a skilled, dedicated professional. Yet all that bending, stretching, and massaging barely made a difference. The tremors and rigidity in Isaak's limbs were getting worse. He saw a neurologist regularly, but without medication little could be done. My husband was growing desperate.

Then in July 1962, hope arrived literally in our mailbox. On the glossy pages of *Look* magazine, we were stunned to see a major article that proclaimed a miracle cure for Parkinson's. It involved a most unusual kind of brain surgery that had already been performed on 170 people, 90 percent of whom reported an end to their symptoms almost immediately.

Look's senior science editor breathlessly told of an operation he had observed led by a medical wunderkind who had worked at the Mayo Clinic and was still in his thirties. Dr. Irving S. Cooper inserted a hollow probe the size of a crochet needle deep into the skull while the patient, given only local anesthesia, remained conscious. When the tip reached a section of the thalamus, about two and half inches inside the brain, Cooper began searching for the nerve cells responsible for the Parkinsonism. In order to find the exact spot, the patient was asked to perform a movement that had been impossible before, such as making a fist or waving a hand. If he could, it meant the right cells had been hit and now they would be frozen and destroyed with liquid nitrogen forced through the needle directly into the area.

Clearly there was no room for even a millimeter of error. The thalamus also controls speech, swallowing, logic, and many other functions that could be impaired by the slightest slip. But the *Look* article stressed the safety of the new technique as well as its effectiveness. "The responsibility of putting in that probe is awesome," solemnly stated Dr. Cooper, originator of this "cryosurgery." He had successfully used chemicals and electrodes in brain surgery before, on patients such as the famous photographer Margaret Bourke-White, but now claimed that the method of freezing was safer.

Isaak was won over not only by the glowing text of the article but also by the incredible photographs. One featured a New Yorker, with the same broad build as my husband, proudly strolling—or, to be more accurate, strutting—in front of his wide-eyed neighbors the day he returned from the hospital. The man had been crippled by Parkinson's his entire adult life and now seemed to radiate good health. Another photo showed him shaving, a task that used to take hours. But now, according to the caption, "Sol Grabino shaves as fast as any man."

Cooper was practicing at St. Barnabus Hospital in the Bronx, and Isaak wanted the operation as soon as it could be scheduled. Both his neurologist and Dr. Julie Stein, having read some questionable assessments of Cooper in the *New York Times* and the professional journals—the word "controversial" was used so often it seemed to be part of his name—opposed the surgery.

I did, too. Obviously, Isaak's present condition was intolerable and could only get worse, but, along with his doctors, I was afraid of such an invasive procedure, only a year old and relatively untested. Could we trust Cooper's claims? I wondered. Even if many of his patients seemed to get better, how did we know their shaking and stiffness wouldn't return? But Isaak wouldn't hear of such doubts. Understandably, he felt he had to take this colossal gamble.

Cooper operated on seven of every ten patients he saw, so Isaak needed a screening appointment consisting of a long series of tests. I went with him. While waiting in the office, I saw something so phenomenal I could barely believe my eyes. A young woman wracked by Parkinson's arrived for surgery, her limbs grotesquely twisted. Yet a few hours later, she walked down the hallway completely normal! Maybe Cooper was some kind of miracle worker after all.

But he was not a mensch. Neither he nor his staff showed us any kindness or compassion, nor did they do anything to relieve our anxiety. The atmosphere in that practice was all business, as cold as the doctor's icy needle. After Isaak was accepted as a candidate, we had to pay $2,000 in advance, and only then did we get to meet the great surgeon. After that one encounter, everything was handled through his office manager or assistants. Most troubling, we got no information on what to expect after the surgery, or what the recovery would be like. None of this gave Isaak any second thoughts, but we had to wait many months anyway because Cooper's calendar was so crowded.

When the big day arrived, Isaak and I got up early and took a taxi to St. Barnabus. As we crossed the city, I looked at the barren trees and gray sky and contemplated the future. He would need me as never before, I knew, and I tried to remain calm and focused. Isaak had sometimes treated me like a child, but now I had to be the strong one.

Yet I nearly lost my composure when I saw him prepped. His scalp was shaven, and a dime-sized hole for the probe had already been drilled into his skull. A cage of metal bands encased his head to hold it steady. Called a "halo," the contraption was screwed into his cranium and looked like a torture device straight out of the Spanish Inquisition. I gasped, and then the doors of the operating room closed behind his gurney.

Awaiting the outcome, I felt utterly alone. Hours went by, and I received no progress reports. Finally, in the late afternoon, a nurse curtly informed me that the surgery was over and I could see my husband. I entered the recovery room and for an instant my spirits rose. He was awake and alert, and his body seemed relaxed. The almost constant shaking on his right side was gone. But I was horrified as soon as he began talking. His voice was loud enough, but I couldn't make out a word, a syllable. The only thing I heard was gibberish.

Was the garbled speech temporary, the result of some pain-killer they'd given him? No, I feared the worst had happened, that the eminent neurosurgeon had missed his mark and damaged a vital part of Isaak's brain.

Frantic for an explanation, I could find no one there to tell me anything. Cooper was long gone, and the doctors who had assisted him had left as well. The nurses and office staff knew nothing.

The only person I could turn to was Julie Stein, who I realized was probably on his way home to Rego Park from his Manhattan office. I also needed to let my family know the results of the operation although I was at a complete loss about what to tell them.

But even getting back home proved an ordeal. In despair about my husband, I was soon also overcome with fear for my physical safety. It was already dark when I exited St. Barnabus, located in a rough neighborhood near the South Bronx. I was afraid to walk the deserted streets to a subway station and then wait on the platform for a train. I'd thought I could just grab a cab, and, as I shivered in the cold, several drivers stopped to pick me up but, afraid they'd get stuck in rush hour traffic, none was willing to take me to Queens. I was trapped in a living nightmare of fright and frustration and I felt abandoned by God and man. Now, as keenly as ever, I felt the loss of my relatives in the Holocaust.

Finally I called Bob Glicken, who mercifully agreed to get in his car and bring me home. But first I had him drop me off at Julie's house. I needed the counsel of an expert and the support of a friend before I could face my kids and my parents.

When I rang the bell, Julie, still wearing his business suit, was finishing dinner with his family, but he got up from the table and ushered me into the living room. All the day's stress boiled over, and I couldn't stop crying as I told him what I'd witnessed. He listened with grave concern and then went to the phone. As a physician he was able to reach a doctor at St. Barnabus familiar with Cooper's method and with my husband's case.

Julie found out that Isaak was probably going to be okay. The unintelligible chatter was likely due to the high fever that a patient often runs when the skull is opened, and indeed his face had been flushed. They'd tried to cool him down with ice packs, we learned, but evidently I'd seen him before his temperature returned to normal. The St. Barnabus doctor added that it was too bad there had been no one around to impart all of this to the patient's wife.

The explanation seemed plausible to Julie, and although I was not convinced, at least I had a shred of hope as I tried to put on a brave face for my family. "Daddy's going to be great," I told the kids, and even forced a smile for them, Tateh, and Mim. But I didn't delude myself; inside, I was more dispirited than ever.

Bella's Sweet Sixteen party was only a week away. I'd known it would coincide with Isaak's return from the hospital, and I figured a nice candlelit Italian dinner for her friends, on checkerboard tablecloths in our finished basement, would work out well. Isaak's head would still be shaved, and I was uncertain about what his physical and mental condition would be. There was even an outside chance he could become loud or violent. So if the gathering were in our home, I thought, he could join in the happy occasion for a while and then simply go up to his bedroom if necessary.

But most of Bella's girlfriends had celebrated their Sweet Sixteens at fancy Midtown hotels, entertained by professional musicians, and, without full knowledge of her father's condition, she had her heart set on doing the same. We didn't want to deny her that happiness, even though it added a lot of work and pressure to one of the most difficult weeks of my life. We also threw a big reception the following year for Paul's bar mitzvah and invited three hundred guests. Caring for Isaak was never my sole responsibility. Both a younger and an older generation depended on me too.

Isaak attended Bella's party at the Gotham Hotel on Fifth Avenue and sat quietly throughout the affair. He was very subdued and hardly talked to anyone. I had brought him home from the hospital a couple of days earlier, and he spoke better than he had during those awful hours following the operation. Even so, he would never be able to articulate his thoughts as before. His speech was slurred, and it got progressively worse—the words more scrambled and the volume weaker—for the rest of his life. For almost two decades after the surgery, his mind functioned well, but because he couldn't express himself properly, people thought him confused. When they asked me what he meant, I wasn't always sure myself, so I'd make up something that fit into the context of the conversation.

I know that gradually losing the power of speech is typical for those with Parkinson's. But because there was such a marked difference right after the operation, I place a lot of the blame on Cooper. Yes, Isaak's tremors abated, but at the price of a clear voice. It was a bad exchange.

Within a few months I went back to Cooper's office on my own to complain about Isaak's muffled speech. I was not permitted to see the doctor, but his office manager told me the problem could be corrected with a second operation, on the other side of Isaak's brain. All we needed to do now was give them another $2,000 and schedule the surgery. "No way!" I answered him sharply. This time, Isaak didn't put up a fight; he never admitted it to me directly, but I think he concluded that Cooper had failed him.

But what was the next step? Someone suggested an entirely different approach—acupuncture. We went to a Korean doctor named Rhee who inserted needles into Isaak's body and head, a frightening sight but a lot less upsetting to me than brain surgery. We went back several times, but Isaak showed no improvement. After that, the only therapy he received was from Bob Glicken, and that, too, was unsuccessful.

Isaak still worked, but by the mid-1960s he couldn't drive anymore. Every day Julie would take Isaak with him to his medical practice on the East Side and then put him in a taxi to the Regent Hotel from there. When Julie moved out of Queens and into Manhattan, I drove Isaak to work, or he went into the city with the Kalts. Sometimes he rode with business partners who were not fully aware of his condition, and he felt humiliated about his growing limitations.

We had heard of research being conducted at the National Parkinson Foundation in Miami. I was so emotionally drained that I couldn't make the Florida trip, but Paul, now a high school student, flew down there with his father to have him examined and see if there were any remedies we had not explored. They stayed in the kosher Sterling Hotel and grew even closer to one another. I was glad that, even under the sad circumstances, they could share that time together. But they returned with no promising news about a cure.

By the late 1960s, Bella was married, working as a speech pathologist, and getting a masters degree at Queens College at night, while Paul was starting Columbia University as an undergraduate. My parents were aging and in bad health, and I, well into my forties, was feeling the march of time myself. I had to face the fact that Isaak might never work again. Few new properties had been acquired since the disease had been diagnosed

Carried aloft in chairs at Bella's wedding.

back in 1960, and his partners thought it was "unsafe" for him to continue managing the Regent, now in a worsening neighborhood. The other owners wanted to buy out my family's sizeable stake in that hotel, our biggest holding. Eventually, we relented.

Luckily, Isaak continued to be insured by the group plan of another of our real estate partnerships; at least his sky-high medical bills would not be a major problem. But how would we be able to pay for everything else? Financial worries kept me awake many a night, even though my father kept reassuring me that we'd be alright. Over the kitchen table, he'd review the family finances and show me the *parnosseh*, as he said in Yiddish, streams of income generated from Isaak's solid investments the decade before. I felt some relief but needed his comfort again and again. Yet, for his sake, I sometimes wished he didn't live so close so he wouldn't constantly have to witness my suffering.

My father died of heart failure in the fall of 1968 at the age of seventy-three. It was especially hard to lose him at a time when the road ahead seemed so difficult. But I was also grateful that he'd been at my side for almost two decades in America and seen his grandchildren reach maturity. He was even able to attend Bella's wedding, although he had endured yet another heart attack just months before. It gave him great joy to be able to nail a mezuzah to the newlyweds' front-door post and to buy me the most beautiful dress I could find for the wedding. I knew I had been lucky; very few of my survivor friends had come out of the fire with a parent. And despite all the barbarity he'd witnessed in his life, he remained a gentle soul until his final day.

My stepmother, Mim, was stricken with uterine cancer a few years after my father passed away. It went into remission after cobalt treatments but then returned. She didn't care for the food at Beth Israel Hospital, so almost daily I'd bring her a thermos of her favorite soup. Fortunately, she went quickly at the end. Although we'd gotten off to a difficult start in Poland, Mim and I had grown very close over the decades. Many people at the shivah, who saw that I wasn't sitting on a low mourner's stool, as a child of the deceased is supposed to do, were surprised to learn I was not her biological daughter. For Paul and Bella, her

My father, in the last months of his life, reciting the blessing over the challah at Bella's wedding, June 9, 1968.

passing was no different than the loss of a beloved grandmother. In fact, throughout most of their childhoods, they thought that the word "Mima" meant grandma, not aunt.

The most positive thing during this period was our discovery of a new neurologist for Isaak, Dr. Melvin Yahr, then in his late forties. He would soon become Mount Sinai Hospital's chairman of neurology and one of the world's leading Parkinson's researchers.

Quiet and reserved, Yahr exhibited little personal warmth (I considered myself lucky if he greeted us by saying hello), yet he was an extraordinary doctor. He was not only a brilliant pioneer in his field, but also exceedingly dedicated to his patients. Whenever I'd bring my husband in for an appointment, and Yahr would notice even a small change in Isaak's condition, he'd berate me for not having reported it to him earlier. Eventually, I established a rapport with Yahr, an American-born Jew, and he sometimes inquired about my trips to Israel. But what counted most was the thorough and advanced medical care he was providing Isaak.

In 1968, Yahr had electrifying news for us. He and some other researchers had just discovered a drug to relieve the symptoms of Parkinson's. Called Levadopa, or simply L-Dopa, it made up for the dopamine deficiency at the root of the disease.

In a healthy person, dopamine is one of the key chemicals in the brain that helps the nerve cells transmit their signals. Parkinson's sets in when, inexplicably, dopamine is no longer naturally produced. Dr. Cooper's method—which Yahr publicly rebuked—had been to penetrate the brain and destroy the cells blocking the manufacture of dopamine. Now a simple pill could be converted by the body into the missing dopamine.

Needless to say, we couldn't wait to get our hands on the magic potion. The only problem was that Mount Sinai was not chosen to be among the first dispensers of L-Dopa, and Dr.

Yahr recommended that I switch to another hospital that could offer the new drug, which also meant another physician. We left Dr. Yahr's practice with deep regret, but in light of the medical breakthrough we felt the change was necessary.

Albert Einstein Medical School was licensed to prescribe the new drug. I went to see the head of the neurology department there, a Dr. Mandel, and was told that the waiting list for L-Dopa was a mile long. I pleaded with him to take pity on Isaak, still a relatively young Parkinson's patient at fifty-three, and Mandel moved him far up the ladder.

We got the medication quickly, and it proved sensational. It was administered gradually, during a hospital stay of several days, but I saw the effects as soon as Isaak ingested the first capsules. Normal movement was restored first to a pinkie, then another finger, then a hand, an arm, and finally his whole right side. I was amazed, and Isaak was euphoric. A day or two later he jumped out of bed and started running around like a hyperactive teenager. A short time after he started taking L-Dopa, we had Paul's friend Sidney, Julie's son, over for Shabbes dinner, and afterward Isaak raced the high school kid home. It wasn't the first instance my husband showed off, but that was one time I could forgive him for it. We thought our eight-year-long ordeal was over.

Our mood was brightened even further because Isaak's friends Ulo Barad and Joe Dunietz had come to the hospital to visit and offered him a marvelous real estate opportunity. They knew nothing of the promise of L-Dopa and hardly expected him to recover. But due to our close personal ties in the past, they invited us take a small position in an art deco icon, the Hotel Edison, a 765-room establishment in the heart of Times Square.

By now, I was making our financial decisions and naturally fretted about depleting my family's cash reserves. So I took only half of what they offered—in hindsight a big mistake, and one for which my husband would never forgive me. But the main thing was that we'd added a fine investment to our portfolio even in the midst of Isaak's illness. To be sure, the Edison had its difficulties as the New York real estate market dipped sharply in the 1970s, but in the end it proved successful.

I wish L-Dopa had performed as well. The terrible problem with the medication, we learned within half a year, is that it wears off. More and more is required to achieve the desired result but that releases too much dopamine and produces horrible side effects—most notably, in Isaak's case, dyskenesia, or wild gyrations of the neck and limbs.

The only remedy is withdrawal, depriving the patient of any and all L-Dopa sometimes for weeks. Known as a "drug holiday," it can be as horrendous as a heroin addict going "cold turkey." Periodically, Isaak had to check into a hospital room to undergo the withdrawal, and once deprived of the medication, he soon lost all control of his body. He couldn't speak, eat, or swallow and had to be fed intravenously. It was one of the most heart-wrenching things I've ever seen: He couldn't even wipe his nose or cover himself.

I pleaded with Dr. Mandel to let me hire a caregiver in the hospital, but he wouldn't allow it. He said he needed to observe what the patient could do for himself without any help. The cycle continued: drug and withdrawal, drug and withdrawal. Finally, Mandel suggested we go back to Dr. Yahr. By then L-Dopa was widely available, and Yahr was the authority in recalibrating the dosage needed as the degenerative disease progressed, a judgment that might reduce the number of fearsome withdrawals.

Yahr prescribed Sinemet, the brand name for L-Dopa, and many other drugs, like Permax, a complimentary medication, which reduced the amount of L-Dopa needed. Isaak also required Deprenyl to inhibit the worst effects of L-Dopa, especially the dyskenesia. Beyond that, he took Zestril for high blood pressure and Zantac for his stomach and wore a nitroglycerine patch, which had to be moved every night, on the left side of his chest near his heart.

From the time Isaak awoke at 8 a.m. until he went to bed at 10 p.m., one or more of the medications had to be administered precisely every two hours. That was my job, and when we went out I always carried a box of pills and a little bottle of water in my purse.

It was a lot of medicine and no doubt contributed to my husband's foggy mental state. But I was grateful that under Dr. Yahr's expert supervision, Isaak's physical deterioration slowed. Throughout the 1970s he was still able to shower and shave on his own.

One symptom, however, grew rapidly worse and worried me to no end: his loss of balance.

Because his reflexes were so compromised, and he couldn't break a fall, his injuries were often severe. He broke his arm, his wrist, his nose. He dislocated his shoulders on several occasions and bloodied his head more times than I can remember. No part of his body escaped punishment.

One of the worst examples occurred when I took him home with me after a routine shopping trip on Austin Street in Forest Hills. He couldn't be in the house alone, so I'd left him in the car while I bought groceries as fast as I could. Afterward, we drove into the garage under our house, and I followed him up the steep stairs to the kitchen, one hand balancing the bundles of food, the other pushing against his back to steady him.

Suddenly, he lost his footing and flipped over my shoulder, fell down the stairs, and hit his head hard against the iron door between the garage and the basement. Blood spurted all over him and onto the floor, a terrifying sight.

I first called my neighbor Hinde Kravitz, a small but strong woman who had been a Bielski partisan. She ran over immediately and was able to drag Isaak from the hallway into the basement and lift him onto a couch. Meanwhile, I made a second call, to Hatzalah, a volunteer ambulance service for the traditional Jewish community. The rescue workers soon arrived and took Isaak and me to the emergency room, where we learned that at least he had not suffered a concussion.

When we got home late that night, the basement was clean. Hinde had mopped the floor while we were away so I wouldn't have to see the blood. The Hatzalah was very considerate, too. They even insisted on bringing us home from the hospital, and I had to force the drivers to accept some money in return. Such decency, from a neighbor and from a communal institution, meant everything to me during an emergency; it reminded me how we all tried to pull together in the shtetl before and during the war.

Unfortunately we had to rely on the services of Hatzalah many times, because Isaak insisted on defying his disability. He had a walker but, out of pride, preferred to use a cane; it often proved no match for a sloping driveway or a wet pavement, and down he'd go.

Even our kitchen could be a perilous place. One time he fell near the counter—I lunged to catch him but just missed—and he dislocated both shoulders, causing him terrific pain. Normally, this would be treated with surgery to repair the ligaments that keep the shoulder in the joint, but Isaak's uncontrolled shaking seemed to rule that out. Although a few surgeons were willing to operate anyway, we kept looking for other answers. Finally, we found the renowned Dr. Bernard Jacobs at the Hospital for Special Surgery on the Upper East Side. He was able, without a scalpel, to maneuver the shoulders back into their cups. He carefully bandaged Isaak and explained that scar tissue would eventually grow around the affected areas and hold the shoulders in place. But only a short while later, at a dinner in my home for close friends from Argentina, he sat down at the table, and somehow all of the doctor's work came undone. Both arms fell out of their sockets, and Isaak screamed in agony. My visitors came to his aid and graciously tried to console me, but I wept openly from the cruelty of this latest blow. He would dislocate his shoulders multiple times and they could never be put back properly.

Of course he was most vulnerable to injury when we went out. Once at a fundraiser for a yeshiva in Jerusalem, held at the Waldorf-Astoria, he fell into a huge potted palm tree, an incident causing both embarrassment and physical pain. After that, whenever we were in a public place, I was afraid to let him out of my sight. If he lingered in the restroom, I feared he'd had some mishap, and I'd stand at the door and ask the men exiting whether they'd seen him and if he was alright. I didn't feel I could relax for one minute.

Trips abroad were especially hazardous, a lesson I learned in Czechoslovakia in the early 1970s. My lower back had been bothering me—a flare-up of the injury I'd suffered as a teenaged forced laborer in the ghetto—and I thought a few weeks at the famous spa at Piestany would do me good. I believed that Isaak, too, could only benefit from the massages and mineral baths. Some friends from New York were on the same trip, and I looked forward to a relaxing, restorative break from my stressful life at home.

But it was not to be. On the day we arrived, as we sat around the pool, Isaak thought he'd be chivalrous and pull over a lounge chair for one of our female friends. Before I could hold him back, he fell flat on his face and bloodied and bruised himself badly. The hospital wasn't far, but I had a lot of trouble getting a taxi to come over and take us. I finally gave up and pushed him in a wheelchair—a long, long way, it turned out, because the spa was on a little island separated from the mainland by two creeks, and the crossing was hundreds of yards away.

Isaak needed plenty of stitches, and for the remainder of the trip I tried to stay as close to him as I could. I enjoyed the healing waters and the rubdowns, but I had to get up at five o'clock for that; from 8 a.m. on I devoted myself to Isaak. Then on our last day at the resort, another crisis. I'd left him sitting safely with lots of people in the garden just long enough to get my hair done but hadn't counted on a sudden squall that sent everyone scurrying indoors. Isaak ran, too—headlong into a giant ornamental elephant at the doorway of the building. The force was so great that he almost split his skull open. This time employees of the spa drove him to the hospital, and a staff member rushed into the beauty parlor to bring me the news. They directed me to wait in my room, and hours later they brought my husband back to me, his head freakishly swollen. He needed an ice pack applied constantly, and that's what I did during the long flight back to New York. As soon as we returned, I had him examined by Julie Stein, who pronounced Isaak fine but lashed out at me for taking him so far from home.

Julie was probably right, but we didn't want Parkinson's to dictate our lives. It may sound reckless, but Isaak and I traveled a lot in the 1970s and '80s, including three trips to Israel—one with my stepmother, one with Paul, and the last time with Paul and his wife, Cheri Forrester, a physician, who helped out a great deal. Paul's Hebrew was fluent, and the family and friends we had there also provided us a bit of security. Not surprisingly, Isaak fell down on several occasions, but the thrill he felt in visiting the Jewish state—a dream since his youth in Poland—was worth it.

He could not join our first family trip to Israel, our bar mitz-

Isaak at the Western Wall.
(Photo by Paul Orbuch)

vah present to Paul in 1964, and I went with both my kids and some lifelong friends. But Isaak wrote a letter to his son in the Holy Land, penning in Hebrew the famous lines of the medieval poet-philosopher Yehuda Ha-Levi: "I am in the west but my heart is in the east." When Isaak did travel with us later, he once went up for an *aliyah* in a synagogue in Herzliya. Walking arm in arm with Paul, he reached the *bimah*, the stage in front of the ark, and sang the blessings over the Torah.

For all of his suffering, Isaak remained deeply involved with his children's lives and was not really depressed even in his final years. Reflecting one of the mysteries of Parkinson's, he could play catch with Paul, sing with gusto in the synagogue, and tinker with some broken household object even while simpler physical tasks proved impossible. Isaak also took a lot of pride in dressing up in elegant suits—a tailor came to our house to fit him—and escorting me to a bar mitzvah or wedding, an organizational fundraiser or installation.

He loved a good joke even if he had to repeat it several times until you got it. Many Parkinson's patients, their muscles rigid, lose the expressiveness in their faces, and he, too, sometimes seemed to be wearing a mask. Yet Isaak could always manage a smile and a chuckle. His name in Hebrew was fitting—it means laughter.

But caring for him took a great toll on me, and even though I found some solace in reading and embroidery, my own health began to show the strain. In the late 1960s my back got so bad I had to wear a tightly laced metal corset. I took medication, too, but was afraid of surgery. When it got to the point that I couldn't get out of bed at night to take Isaak to the bathroom, I hired a Russian émigré named Boris to do it. He slept in my bed next to Isaak. Paul was now grown up and out of the house, so I recuperated in his room. I took a liking to Boris, who held a doctorate in mathematics from a Soviet university and was struggling to support his wife and baby. But when my back improved, I sent him home.

My privacy was important to me, and I resisted getting permanent live-in help as long as I could. Bella, though, was always concerned about the sacrifices I was making and insisted we convert the basement into a room for a caregiver. In the late 1980s, almost three decades after Isaak's diagnosis, I gave in and hired an attendant.

These jobs are usually performed by new immigrants, and I figured the best choice would be a Polish woman, with whom I could converse in her native language, and who would be familiar with the kind of food we ate. Since then, for caregivers or housekeepers, I've always tried to hire Poles. It was hard for me to live with a stranger, but there was one big upside: I finally had the freedom to go out when I pleased.

A few years later we took another major step and sold our

Isaak outside our home in the Crescents of Rego Park, Queens.
(Photo by Paul Orbuch)

house in the Crescents, filled with so many memories, both happy and tragic, and moved to the Bay Area. Paul, now a corporate executive, and Bella, a well-known local publisher and restaurant writer, had both been living north of the Golden Gate Bridge in Marin County, and we naturally wanted to be closer to them as I entered my mid-sixties and Isaak his mid-seventies.

Even while we still lived in New York, we had flown to California a couple of times a year and stayed with Bella and her second husband and business partner, Dan Whelan. Together they had founded and continued to publish the popular *In-Room Cityguide to the San Francisco Bay Area and Northern California*. Often they invited us to join them in Lake Tahoe or Carmel. Other times, leaving Isaak with Paul, I accompanied them to Hawaii and Mexico, and later Thailand, Singapore, and Bali, places I probably never would have visited on my own.

197

I was initially hurt by Bella's marriage to a non-Jew in 1978, but Dan won me over not only with his deep respect for Judaism but also because of his unflagging devotion to Isaak. He patiently listened to my husband's rambling stories, proudly introduced him to top restaurant owners, and dutifully assisted him in getting to the bathroom. It meant a lot to me.

My kids helped us find and move into a pleasant townhouse in suburban Corte Madera. Leaving my many close friends and my Jewish charitable work behind was exceedingly difficult. I could never replicate the elaborate web of connections I had in New York, a network of people and organizations I'd maintained even in the worst times of Isaak's illness.

Gradually, though, I made a new life for myself on the West Coast. I found a new soul mate, my neighbor Ida Gelbart, a Holocaust survivor from Poland. Her husband suffered from Parkinson's for seventeen years, so, like me, she was a battle-scarred veteran of two wars. Our families celebrated every holiday together as one big family.

I soon joined the board of the Marin chapter of Hadassah, where I helped plan some of its events and activities while making new friends. Isaak and I also joined a Conservative synagogue, and it turned out that its inspiring rabbi, Lavey Derby, was Paul's schoolmate at Ramaz, a Jewish high school in Manhattan, and the son of the rabbi who had performed Bella's first marriage back in Forest Hills in the late 1960s. In Corte Madera I would eventually look back on my long, hard life, and try to understand it.

Yet nothing has come close to the satisfaction and joy I've received from my only grandchild, Paul's daughter, Eva, born in 1989. For Isaak and me to witness the beginning of a new generation of our family was a wonder beyond words.

By the time Eva was born, Isaak required more care than

he could get at home. I still conferred with Dr. Yahr about his medication, but the drugs were having less and less effect. Now there was little my husband could do on his own. I helped him with his morning shower, and we had a live-in attendant for his other needs, but his body and his mind were failing.

Like many spouses in this situation, I resisted putting him in an institution. After four and a half decades of marriage, I wanted to continue living with him; otherwise I knew we'd both feel terribly unnatural and alone. But again Bella thought differently. She strongly felt it would be best for Isaak, and the rest of the family too, if he were in a health care facility, and Paul soon agreed.

My kids took me to one place after another, and I rejected them all, until I visited the "Rolls Royce of nursing homes," as they put it, the Tamalpais, in the nearby town of Greenbrae. This one seemed superbly run, with about the same number of patients as staff members. It was one of the hardest things I've ever had to do, but I agreed to entrust them with my frail husband.

I quickly saw I had made the right choice. But even though Isaak was in one of the best facilities available, we arranged for another layer of care, a personal nurse. Bronia, originally from a small town near Krakow, was my live-in housekeeper, but during the day she stayed with and cared for Isaak. I drove her to the nursing home every morning, where she fed him breakfast, dressed and groomed him, and wheeled him out to the garden. She sat with him there, fed him lunch, and then took him back to his room for a nap. In the afternoon, she repeated the routine. One of the problems of advanced Parkinson's is heavy perspiration, and Bronia frequently changed his shirt and handkerchief; the new ones were always of pure white cotton, perfectly laundered and starched.

I visited for several hours every day and evening, and Paul,

With our granddaughter, Eva Orbuch.
(Photo by Paul Orbuch)

Bella, and Dan came often too. We sometimes took Isaak out of the Tamalpais for a change of scenery. Eva, now starting school, raised his spirits the most. His eyes lit up when she sang *Yismechu Hashamayim*, a Hebrew melody that put him in touch with his own childhood. The title means "May the Heavens be Joyful."

By 1997 Isaak was dying. He could barely swallow, and then he contracted pneumonia. The prognosis was grim, but I wasn't going to give up now. I insisted the doctors fight the infection with antibiotics. The pills had to be pulverized first, put into ice cream, and spoon-fed to him by Bronia with the greatest difficulty.

He struggled up to the very end, but I think something my son said finally allowed Isaak to let go. Paul was the last of us to see him alive: "Dad, it's okay. You've been a fighter. You've done a fine job and left us in good shape." As Isaak would have wanted at his funeral, we all sang *Yismechu Hashamayim*.

Epilogue

THERE'S A SAYING THAT FITS my life in America: "The past is never dead and buried. It isn't even past." I've lived sixty years in the New World, but in many ways I've never left the Old. Every day my heart aches from the loss of my mother and two brothers, dozens of other relatives, and nearly all of my childhood friends. I've keenly felt their absence at every stage of my adult life: in times of joy when I married and had children, in times of sadness when I grappled with my husband's illness and death.

With the friendship of other survivors and their families, first in New York and then in California, I've tried to recreate the sense of kinship and caring I knew in prewar Luboml. But nothing can ever replace what was taken from me. I've been responding to my loss ever since.

I never visited Luboml after immigrating to America, as some survivors did. I knew that no Jews remained there, and I simply couldn't bear to set foot on those blood-soaked streets

In my home in Corte Madera, California. (Photo by Evvy Eisen)

again. Neither of my kids has gone either. But the repercussions of the Holocaust have brought Poland and Ukraine to me.

As early as the 1950s, Isaak and I struggled with the moral question of whether or not to apply for reparations from the West German government. The permanent injury to my spine, incurred when the Nazis forced me to work on the train tracks, plus the constant mental anguish I'd endured since 1941, entitled me to a modest monthly stipend. I knew it would require a grueling application process, including humiliating visits to German lawyers and psychologists, and my first inclination was to forego this "opportunity."

I also felt it was blood money the Germans were offering, an easy way for the killers to lessen their guilt and return to the family of civilized nations. They called it *Wiedergutmachung*, or "making it good again." But how could they compensate me for the murder of my loved ones? For depriving me of a normal youth and education? For imprisoning and terrorizing my family and me in our hometown?

After much discussion, Isaak persuaded me to think about it differently. If you don't want to spend the money, he argued, then give it away and let it do some good; nothing will be gained if Bonn keeps it. I finally saw his point, and once I received my first check I set up a pattern I follow to this day: every penny goes into a separate account and is donated to a Jewish organization. Over the years it's come to many thousands of dollars—for yeshivas, synagogues, Zionist causes, and Holocaust remembrance—and I feel I did the right thing.

Accepting restitution, however, did not mean forgiveness on my part toward the Germans, Poles, or Ukrainians. In 1963, my family and I were outraged to learn that two individuals responsible for the annihilation of Luboml's Jews were living in Philadelphia, less than a hundred miles from us. The brothers Sergei and Mikolay Kowalchuk, like so many other perpetrators of the Final Solution, had made false statements on their visa applications to enter the United States after the war and lied again in their naturalization papers. They were now American citizens, living quietly under their real names with their wives and children in the City of Brotherly Love. Ironically, they both worked as tailors in a shop owned by a Jew.

They had first been exposed by a Soviet newspaper, which identified Sergei as Luboml's former chief of police, who, in October 1942, had organized the roundup of thousands of Jews for the SS executioners while looting Jewish property in the process. The younger Mikolay, also a policeman, was one of his accomplices. Tateh believed that Mikolay was the same Ukrainian we encountered the night of our escape from the ghetto, who had let us pass only after accepting the bribe of "dollars" from my father and the wedding ring from my mother, although I couldn't be sure.

The *New York Times* soon ran a story about the Soviet allegations, and pressure began to build for a U.S. government inquiry. A number of our friends from Luboml, such as Nathan Sobel, sent eyewitness accounts of the Kowalchuks' savagery to officials in Washington, D.C. Such cases were then handled by the INS, and for many years no action was taken against the brothers.

Things changed in the late 1970s, however, when the hunt for Nazis and their collaborators living in America was entrusted to a new Office of Special Investigations under the auspices of the Justice Department. There was more evidence against Sergei than Mikolay, so the government targeted the older Kowalchuk first, opening proceedings in 1977 to strip him of his citizenship, a prelude to deportation. Our friend Abe Getman testified at length when the trial was finally held four years later in the federal courthouse in Philadelphia. Moishe Lifshitz, married to my second cousin Chanah, felt so strongly about bringing Kowalchuk to justice that he journeyed from Israel several times to be a witness. He and Chanah stayed in our home during those visits, and Isaak and I admired his determination.

Sergei's citizenship was finally revoked in 1983, and three years later the government moved to deport him. But by then he had vanished, and has not been heard from since. Sadly, the government lost the case it brought against Mikolay, and he was allowed to remain in Philadelphia. We didn't have the satisfaction of seeing the Kowalchuks kicked out of the country, but at least we know their lives were disgraced and disrupted.

While I had a front-row seat to the punishment of a perpetrator, I was much more intent on rewarding a rescuer. That took even longer. As soon as we got settled in the DP camp, my father and I tried to get in touch with Tichon, the peasant who had been our guardian angel in the forest. We hadn't seen him since my days at the Luboml post office in late 1944 and wanted to let him know we were alive and well, and forever grateful. I didn't even know his last name, but my father remembered it: Martynetz.

Sadly, my many letters from the American zone of occupation to his remote village, now in the Ukrainian Republic of the Soviet Union, were returned unopened. The envelope was stamped in Russian: "No one of that name at this address." Having myself been a postal worker in the USSR, I surmised it was too dangerous for Tichon to receive mail from a DP camp run by the U.S. Army.

I thought my relatives in Argentina might have a better chance to contact him, and I sent them the Martynetz's address. In the same letter in which I joyfully announced Bella's birth, I urged them to inform Tichon about Tateh's and my fortunate circumstances and send his family a gift of appreciation. "I have a favor to ask," I wrote to Buenos Aires, "You know how we survived. Some people helped us; these people should be given some help." But they also received no response.

It took more than half a century, but with luck I finally made contact with Tichon's family. One night in the late 1990s, I described at length to my housekeeper, an immigrant from Warsaw, how we survived in the forest. When I told her about Tichon's good deeds and my fruitless attempts to locate him, she asked me where he lived. Coincidentally, she had a cousin in that very region, a reliable female attorney whom I could hire to track down the Martynetz family.

Within a short time, my private investigator found out Tichon's fate, and I was heartbroken by the news. He had died in prison in 1961 in Kharkov, hundreds of miles from his home and family, at the end of a decade-long sentence for propagating Ukrainian nationalism. The soulless Soviet officials never even returned the body to the family for proper burial. His wife, Fedora, passed away ten years later.

My contact in Ukraine first found Tichon's son, Alexei, born after the war and living near his father's tiny village in northwest Volhynia, and then his two daughters. Oksana Tichonovna was the woman who, as a teenaged girl, had often walked into the woods with her parents to bring us pirogi, vodka, and sometimes bread. When I was finally able to talk to her by phone from California, I was convinced it was the same person. She reminded me that I'd once given her a skirt and even recalled the color, and she remembered my father's name in Ukrainian—Wolko.

Now that I knew it was the right family, I immediately sent gifts to all three of Tichon's children. The daughters, then in their seventies and in poor health, soon passed away; but I remained in touch with Oskana's daughter, Ludmilla, and told her how her grandfather had saved four Jewish lives during the war. It has been my privilege to assist that family over the years.

Aside from the material help to Ludmilla and her fine family, I felt it was important to recognize publicly Tichon's kindness and courage. I wanted all of his descendents to know that even though he had died in jail he was a hero. So I contacted the head of the American Society for Yad Vashem, Eli Zborowski, who himself had been saved by Poles during the Holocaust.

Eli was a longtime family friend who belonged to our synagogue in Forest Hills and whose daughter had been Paul's schoolmate. Isaak and I had been among his earliest supporters when he began raising funds for Yad Vashem in the 1960s. Now in 2000, with his encouragement, I wrote a long letter attesting to Tichon's altruism and sent it to Jerusalem. The following year, he was honored posthumously as one of the Righteous Among the Nations. A ceremony was held in his village, and the Israeli Consul General came from Lvov to participate. Tichon's family was so moved they've erected a monument to him. It is the very least he deserves.

I also wanted the facts of my family's survival and Tichon's goodness to be known on this side of the Atlantic, especially by younger people. But in the first decades after the war it was hard for me to speak of the traumatic events I'd endured. I unburdened myself only to a small circle of fellow survivors, and even then I related only bits and pieces of what had happened.

Yet in 1970, I was called upon to bear witness in an unlikely place—Argentina. I visited the families of my mother's two brothers who had emigrated from Poland well before the war and now lived in Lanus, a Buenos Aires suburb. My Argentine uncles, both still alive, had seven children among them, my only first cousins, who, of course, had children of their own. About twenty people from this clan met me at the airport, and though the weather was cold—I'd left New York in the summer and encountered the South American winter—my relatives treated me with great warmth.

They belonged to a synagogue and were avid Zionists and proud Jews. Above all, they wanted to learn the fate of the family and town that had been left behind. The Yizkor Buch, or memorial book, on Luboml, containing dozens of articles, including three by my father, would answer many of their questions, but it would not be published for several years.

Of course, the Argentine branch of the family was aware of the overall destruction wrought by the Nazis. As early as 1946 I had written them that all that remained in Luboml was "debris and graves...and memories." I knew it would cause them unbearable pain, but I had to pen the words that nearly everyone in the family had been murdered, "that the light had gone out for me." Now, a quarter century later, I would give them the specifics.

I don't think I've ever talked as much in my life. Every day from morning until night, my uncles, aunts, and cousins gathered around, filled with curiosity but also dread about what they were about to find out. We cried a lot but also felt pride as I told them in Yiddish of the heroism of Shneyer and Meir and above all Uncle Hershel—so lovingly remembered by his brothers—who had lost everything, yet kept my parents and me alive through a brutal winter. I explained how the Jewish quarter of Luboml had been burned to the ground, how we cowered in fear in the ghetto, and how the Jews had been executed in front of graves they'd been forced to dig themselves.

But at least a few of us had fled into the forest and fought back with the partisans, I let them know. Sitting with my relatives, there were some light moments too, as we recounted the antics of the colorful characters of our prewar shtetl. I felt great responsibility as sole survivor of my mother's large family, a kind of storytelling emissary to those who had gotten out before the catastrophe.

Paul also visited our Argentine relatives, in 1974 at the end of a year-and-a-half-long trip by jeep he and a buddy took through Latin America, an extended break from his studies at Columbia. In a suburb of Cordoba, he knocked on the door of my cousin Marcos, a university professor, and was treated with the same wonderful hospitality that I'd enjoyed four years earlier. Paul, who had learned Spanish with the goal of this visit in mind, established strong bonds with that family and with the many relatives he visited in Lanus before returning to the States. We've remained in touch with them and Paul hopes to bring my granddaughter to Argentina to meet them in the near future.

The Argentine connection forced me to articulate my story, but except for family members and close friends it remained locked inside me for many years thereafter. As more about the Holocaust emerged in American culture—memoirs and novels, films and television shows—I sometimes felt that, not having been in a concentration camp, I hadn't suffered as much as others, and that my experience was therefore not as worthy.

Beyond that, I was preoccupied with Isaak's illness and the needs of others in my family and had little time or energy for anything else. To delve into my past, I knew, would be deeply disturbing and all-consuming. I didn't even submit an article for the Luboml Yizkor Buch, which appeared in Yiddish and Hebrew in 1975. With great reluctance, I agreed to a tape-recorded interview by a graduate student in the late 1980s and two videotaped oral histories in the following decade, but I always shied away from appearing before a live audience. Yes, back in New York I had spoken frequently for Hadassah on the great work it was doing in Israel. But talking about my own life was another matter entirely.

All that changed around the turn of the new century, when with more time for reading, reflection, and travel to such destinations as St. Petersburg and Prague, I realized that internment in a camp was hardly a prerequisite for speaking as a survivor. Rather, I now wanted people to consider the partisans as they pondered the destruction of European Jewry. The story of my family—every member of which fought back in one way or

On a Baltic cruise.
(Photo by Paul Orbuch)

another—would provide a much fuller picture of the Jewish response to the Holocaust.

In the spring of 2001, my dear friend and neighbor Ida Gelbart recommended me as the keynote speaker for Marin's community-wide Yom Ha-Shoah commemoration. It would be the most elaborate event of its kind ever held in our county. When the invitation came from Rachel Biale, the director of adult education at the Osher Marin Jewish Community Center, I expressed my ambivalence about revealing my life story to a gathering of hundreds of people. But she had confidence that I would make a deep impact on the audience and persuaded me to accept.

I prepared a straightforward narrative of my youth in Europe, emphasizing my year with the partisans, and Paul and Bella helped me edit it. I was nervous before I spoke, but my son steadied me with words of love and encouragement, and I believe my talk was well received.

Around that time a young local filmmaker named Mitch Braff was embarking on an ambitious project of preserving former partisans' stories on videotape. He heard of my speech at the JCC

*With my son, Paul Orbuch, in the library of Congregtion Kol Shofar
before my presentation at a Yom Ha-Shoah commemoration.*

from Rabbi Stacy Friedman of Congregation Rodef Sholom, who had been in the audience that day, and Mitch soon contacted me. I was privileged to be the first of many dozens of former partisans from all over the world that he would interview.

When he came to my home and set up his equipment for the day-long taping, Paul was impressed with his professionalism, and we both decided to support his efforts. Before long, Paul joined the board of Mitch's fledgling Jewish Partisan Educational Foundation, devoted to developing and disseminating educational materials on the young Jews who fought back during the war. In 2004, Paul became president of the fast-growing JPEF, and along with the philanthropist Elliott Felson, also the son of a local partisan, he serves as co-president today.

Through JPEF and other sources, I've received numerous speaking engagements, and it would become easier each time I addressed a new group. At a JPEF event in 2006, I participated in a program in front of nearly five hundred people. I was introduced by the actor Ed Asner and was interviewed on stage by the noted Holocaust scholar Michael Berenbaum.

A panel discussion presented by the Jewish Partisan Educational Foundation at the Jewish Community Center San Francisco in 2006. From left to right, Michael Berenbaum, former Czechoslovak partisan Martin Petrasek, myself, and Ed Asner, whose cousin was a partisan. (Photo by Paul Orbuch)

Today, I most enjoy talking to youth groups and have spoken in libraries and schools both to Jewish and non-Jewish students throughout the San Francisco Bay Area. Their queries range from the most practical—How did girls deal with their periods in the forests?—to the most philosophical—How is it possible to believe in God after Hitler?

I do not take it upon myself to impart theology to the school kids. All I tell them is that I don't have any answers, only more questions.

Frequently I ask myself: If there is a God, why has He punished me so severely? I am referring not only to the Shoah. Until now I've never shared the story of Isaak's illness publicly, but in truth I've been the victim of both moral evil at the hands of the Nazis and natural evil in the form of Parkinson's. In some ways my husband's disease wounded me even more deeply than did my wartime experiences. Of course I sustained incalculable losses in Europe, but as a partisan I was engaged in a noble struggle, not only to survive but also to defeat tyranny and create a new world. It was a war between good and evil, and I had countless comrades along the way. Again and again I was kept alive through the help of others.

Teaching a seminar of honors students at the Holocaust Center of Northern California in San Francisco. (Photo by Paul Orbuch)

Perhaps that trial by fire steeled me for the ordeal that came later, lasting more than a third of a century. I wouldn't yield to the ravages of the disease any more than I'd be passive in the face of fascism.

But that second war was a lonelier struggle against a more mysterious foe. I could contend with a difficult doctor or an imperfect drug, but the true enemy lurked deep within my husband's body and brain, and it struck randomly. In my darkest moments his affliction even drained the meaning from the valiant years of my youth. Had I endured the Holocaust when I was young, I wondered, only to be plagued in a different way when I was older?

Yet, with the benefit of hindsight I've gained in my ninth decade, I now feel much more hope than despair. Because I survived the war while so many perished, and because so many of the survivors have passed on, I savor each day as a special gift. I've witnessed the rebirth of Israel and participated in robust Jewish communities in New York and California. Most rewarding of all, I've seen my children and granddaughter thrive in America.

In the way they lead their lives I've observed how they've been uplifted by even the most harrowing of Isaak's and my experiences. The past has been a gift to them more than it has been a burden. Paul expressed it well when he followed my speech at the Jewish Community Center in 2001 with his own remarks. He mentioned sadness for our great loss, the grandmother, aunts, uncles, and cousins he never knew.

But overall, his message was positive: "I came to appreciate the tremendous strength it took for the survivors to carry on after the war," he said. "It was so important for them to return to normalcy and even in the difficult circumstances of the DP camps to set up schools and cultural centers, to have kids as soon as they could. But they did a great deal more than carry on in their new countries; they thrived...These people had seen their entire way of life destroyed, yet look what they have recreated in its place."

From his parents' life stories, he has also gained compassion, and it goes beyond his remarkable devotion to me in my old age; it extends to his friends, his acquaintances, even strangers. Like Ida Gelbart's son, Sam, whose father was also a longtime Parkinson's sufferer, Paul has developed a sixth sense for knowing how to come to the aid of a disabled individual. Once when my son was given the honor of carrying the Torah through the aisles of our synagogue, he led the procession to the area where people were sitting in wheelchairs—I don't know if anyone had ever done that before—and the incapacitated folks were thrilled with the opportunity to touch and kiss the holy scroll. It was an act of kindness he would have wanted someone to perform for his own father.

Eva, meanwhile, has shown me the effect I've had upon the third generation of my family. In 2007, I did not participate in Marin County's annual Yom Ha-Shoah commemoration—I had been on the program each year since my maiden voyage—but I sat in the audience and heard her share the perspective of a grandchild of survivors. She was very familiar with my past, having heard stories over Shabbes dinner almost every week from the time she was a little girl. Now at seventeen she was the same age as me when I fled the ghetto for the forests and joined the partisans.

She stated the obvious differences between herself, "now fretting over college choices," and her grandma, who as a teenager "was carrying hand grenades on missions." But Eva also explained that in her own way she was continuing our family tradition of defying oppression. She described a panel she'd organized in her high school, in which she'd recruited a Sudanese refugee to raise

With Eva. (Photo on the left by Paul Orbuch, on the right by Bruce Forrester)

awareness about the genocide in Darfur. "We Jews have gone through so much hardship," she told everyone, "it is our responsibility to take action as early as possible against other injustices in the world."

With enormous pride I've seen her develop a theater workshop for teens on Middle East peace, organize an elaborate event at her high school for World AIDS Day, and lead demonstrations against global poverty. Along with other young people she went to Washington to lobby Congress to do more for universal primary education overseas, and spent a winter break in New Orleans helping to rebuild houses damaged by Hurricane Katrina.

I don't know if I deserve all the credit Eva gives me for providing her, as she says, with the "strength and inspiration" for her struggle against intolerance and injustice. But her sensitivity to the suffering of others and her spirit of resistance have given me reason to believe that the lessons of my life will resonate long after I'm gone.

On that spring day in 2007 she was the one who gave me strength and inspiration by quoting the saying of the nineteenth-century Chasidic Rabbi Menachem Mendel of Kotsk: "There is nothing so whole as a broken heart."

Afterword and Acknowledgments

I FIRST MET SONIA ORBUCH at an event launching my book *Taking Risks*, co-authored with Joseph Pell (RDR Books/Magnes Museum, 2004). In that memoir, I helped Joe recount his story of fleeing his shtetl on the eve of its liquidation by the Germans and fighting back from the forests with the Soviet partisans.

After speeches by Joe, Professor David Biale, and me, Sonia rose to her feet. "I salute you as a fellow partisan," she announced, and then introduced herself to the audience. As she spoke about her wartime experience, I was impressed by her rare blend of confidence and humility, knowledge and curiosity.

Working with Joe, I had become engrossed in the partisan saga and wanted to research and write the "woman's story" as well. Fortuitously, Sonia was finally ready to delve into her past, and she and her son, Paul, having read *Taking Risks*, entrusted me with the responsibility of helping to shape her recollections into the foregoing narrative.

We three sat together for a series of interviews in Sonia's Corte Madera home, coincidentally only a few miles from San Rafael, where I'd interviewed Joe several years before. Their partisan brigades, too, had operated in close proximity to one another more than sixty years earlier in north central Volhynia.

But while Joe Pell's life in America has been an upward trajectory marked by immense success, fate was less kind to Sonia. Although her husband, Isaak, was initially pointed toward prominence in the New York hotel business, his tragic illness sidelined him for the last thirty-seven years of his life. Sonia was drawn into a second war, against Parkinson's disease, for her personally an ordeal perhaps even more devastating than the Holocaust.

At first, I wondered whether such an outcome would leave the reader and me downcast. But in the end, I found Sonia's story uplifting, too. Like Joe, the traits she brought with her to America served her well even, and especially, in times of crisis. Sonia, I came to understand, is a prime example of the "woman of valor" of which the Book of Proverbs speaks.

IN PLACING SONIA'S LIFE IN historical context I was aided by many publications, most notably the Yizkor Buch, *Luboml: The Memorial Book of a Vanished Shtetl* (Ktav, 1997; Yiddish/Hebrew edition, 1975). I am grateful to Berl Kagan, Nathan Sobel, Aaron Ziegelman and many others for compiling this invaluable record of their town, and I gained much from the accounts of Moishe Lifshitz, Rochl Lachter, Yisroel Lachter, and especially Sonia's father, Wolf Shainwald. Also helpful was the memoir of Luboml native Abraham Getman, *Borders of Hope* (Vantage, 2000).

For the chapter on the Soviet occupation of eastern Poland, I learned a great deal from Jan T. Gross's *Revolution from Abroad* (Princeton, 1998, 2000). On the period following the German invasion of Sonia's region, there is no substitute for Shmuel Spector's *Holocaust of Volhynian Jews, 1941–1944* (Yad Vashem, 1990), which includes a reference to Sonia's brother Meir Shainwald as a partisan. I also consulted Reuben Ainsztein's comprehensive *Jewish Resistance in Nazi-occupied Eastern Europe* (P. Elek, 1975), Nechama Tec's *Defiance: The Bielski Partisans* (Oxford, 1993), and her *Resilience and Courage: Men, Women and the Holocaust* (Yale, 2003).

Researching the post-liberation period, I benefited from Yehuda Bauer's *Flight and Rescue: Bricha* (Random House, 1970) and another work by the brilliant Jan T. Gross, *Fear: Anti-Semitism in Poland after Auschwitz* (Random House, 2006). Regarding the DP camps, I studied an important collection of letters by a young American social worker, Oscar A. Mintzer, *In Defense of the Survivors* (Magnes Museum, 1999) and Zeev Mankowitz' monograph *Life between Memory and Hope* (Cambridge, 2002). Of greatest value was the biography of Sonia's close friend Nathan Baruch, *Battling for Souls*, by Alex Grobman (Ktav, 2004), who also

Sonia Shainwald Orbuch and Fred Rosenbaum. (Photo by Paul Orbuch)

granted me an informative interview. On the life of Holocaust survivors in the United States, William B. Helmreich's *Against all Odds* (Simon and Schuster, 1992) was highly illuminating.

In order to grasp the agony of Parkinson's disease and its impact on the victims' loved ones, I was aided by two celebrity memoirs, *Lucky Man* by Michael J. Fox (Hyperion, 2002) and *Saving Milly* by Morton Kondracke (Public Affairs, 2001). I also consulted the more clinical *A Life Shaken* by Joel Haverman (Johns Hopkins, 2002) and the autobiography of Isaak's brain surgeon, I.S. Cooper, *The Vital Probe* (Norton, 1981).

In addition to these printed materials, I drew upon an audio-taped interview of Sonia in 1988 by Carol Linker, an Orbuch family friend and graduate student, and two extensive video-taped oral histories. The first was conducted in December 1994, by Sandra Bendayan for San Francisco's Holocaust Oral History Project. The second was done in May 1998 by Yvonne Walter for the Survivors of the Shoah Visual History Project based in Los Angeles. Of great help as well were the interviews and images of Sonia and other partisans provided by Mitch Braff and his staff at the Jewish Partisan Educational Foundation.

In early 2008, just as Sonia and I were completing our manuscript, I was jolted by the news of a source that could potentially shift much of the story. Paul learned that a trove of more than a hundred letters, written by the Shainwald, Lachter, and Orbuch families in the 1930s and '40s, including several by Sonia herself, lay in a closet in a Buenos Aires suburb. The dispatches had been sent from Europe to Sonia's uncles and aunts who had immigrated to Argentina before the war. Thankfully, they had been held in safekeeping for decades by Sonia's niece Sheive (Silvia) Lachter Borenstein. Paul arranged for the letters to be copied and sent to him and he engaged both Yiddish and Russian translators to render them into English. Remarkably, the missives were not

Sonia studying the letters from the 1930s and '40s recently found in Argentina.
(Photo by Paul Orbuch)

mentioned by her relatives when Sonia visited in 1970.

I was intensely curious about their contents. Would they provide fresh vignettes and more texture to the overall story? Might they cast a new light on the portraits of Sonia and her family that I had drawn?

As it turned out, many of these messages from a vanished world were simply perfunctory greetings of little historical or biographical import. Others did offer some new details, which I incorporated into the text. But most striking was the congruity between Sonia's written record of more than six decades ago and her spoken recollections of 2005–2008. Her letters of 1946 and 1947 from the Zeilsheim DP camp, which appear in the appendix, prove that for her very little has dimmed over time.

I would like to thank those who read all or part of the manuscript in its various stages and gave us helpful suggestions and warm encouragement: Dorothy Shipps, Julie Cohen, Roger

Rapoport, Harold Lindenthal, Vivien Orbach, Cheri Forrester, Lisa Paul King, Mitch Braff, Robert E. Shepard, Rob Monyak, who also translated several of the Russian letters and poems as did Tatyana Yurkhova, and of course the preeminent Holocaust scholar Michael Berenbaum who wrote the foreword. Sonia's daughter, Bella Orbuch Whelan, carefully edited the entire book and improved it markedly as did the copyeditor Richard Harris. This volume owes much to Eric Triantafillou's keen eye for design. My sister, Bobbi Leigh Zito, suggested the unusual title.

Above all, my thanks go to Paul Orbuch, co-president of the Jewish Partisan Educational Foundation. He enthusiastically participated in every interview, read much of the secondary literature in the field, and brought important sources to my attention. His input was essential not only to the content and style of the text but also to the images and design of the volume. Neither Sonia nor I can imagine having written this book without him.

Fred Rosenbaum
Berkeley, California
Brooklyn, New York

Appendix

1. Poem by Piotr Menaker, 8/31/1943, original in Russian.

We are now sitting
           Together
Without saying a
           word
I am thinking only about
When will we meet again?
I dream of sitting
           alone with you
Embracing tenderly
So that you can tell me
About love and encounters
           long passed.
I would like to give you
           a hug
And to explain myself with
           A hot kiss.
Love without a kiss
           Will not endure.
So don't be shy to kiss me and to be
           Tender with me
Because of love and good friendship.
           Nature will forgive.
We inhale nature
           Take all...
While the heart still breathes.

August 31, 1943
Forest Or. Vo.

2. Poem by Piotr Menaker, 9/15/1943, original in Russian.

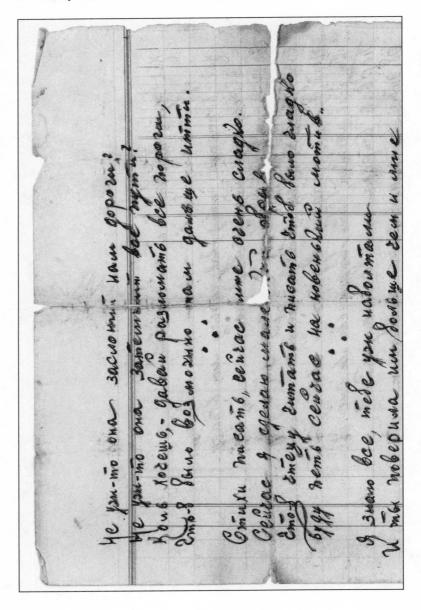

The sound of your voice is the pleasing sound of a guitar
When I try to remember how we sat in the forest in the shade of a pine tree
Sonia! I still remember our encounters...
Which remain with me forever.
There is nothing in the world, which would be sweeter than that,
If it exists somewhere it is only in a dream.
The first encounter was accidental
We didn't see it coming
I had to talk to you with desperation
We had to reach an agreement once and for all.
You didn't say many words of love,
But without words you let me understand,
That you fell in love with me in the same way I did with you
Then I had enough courage to embrace you.
Oh, Sonia, my thoughts about you are so beautiful.
It is such a pleasure to remember them, but my heart is aching.
Sonyichka, remember those clear nights!
It is not good what your mom said.
It is very strange what happened with us.
Whom should we blame? Perhaps myself.
I opened up my weak heart
And out poured all its love on you .
You may judge me, Sonyichka, as you please,
I will accept your verdict as final
I am sure that you know my thoughts
And I will keep them forever.
Know that I am not going to compliment you anymore
And I do not want to praise myself.
I don't know what step to take,
How will we meet again?
When your mother stands in our way.
I can't believe she is going to stop us!
I can't believe she will obscure our path!
We could break all obstacles if you want to,
That way it will be possible for us to go together further.

      • •

I write my poetry and it feels sweet.
I am going to cut this off now and make a small change of course
For my reader to have more pleasure and to make it easier to read
I am going to sing with a different tune

• •
•

I know all the slander they whispered in your ear
And you believed them more than you believed me
They probably lost their mind from envy
And this silly nonsense got into you.
But I have said enough about it.

Sonia, you spilled enough tears about that
Those were times when we were joking
And finally it is time for you to think and talk seriously.
Only if you wish we could have our encounters again
And resist the words of our enemies
If you do not want it you just need to tell me one word.
And we will take different paths for many years.

Let the Nudieski forest remember about the past...
Let the Lubieshovski forest cry its tears about it...
Let our enemies suffer from bad luck
And then Piotr Menaker will be watching.
I am writing this poetry in Kochotske-Vola
My thoughts are stretching to the Lubieshovski forest
What kind of fortune will I have?
Will I advance or fall back?

3. Postcard sent by Sonia from post-liberation Luboml, 10/8/44, original in Russian

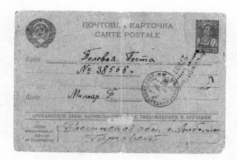

Front Side:
Military post, free mailing #38568
(Translator's note: Military post offices had numbers instead of mailing addresses, for security reasons. Note the round hand stamp. This is a military post office stamp, and above it is another one, which says: "Checked by Military Censorship 278337." Every piece of military mail was checked for sensitive information.)

To: B. Miller

Rossinsky District, town Luboml
Town Soviet (Municipal Office)

Back Side:
This is in answer to your letter. Your relatives whom you are asking about in your letter do not live in the city of Luboml anymore.

/Secretary of Town Soviet/signature

4. Sonia's letter to her relatives in Argentina from the Zeilsheim DP camp.
7/21/1946 , original in Polish.

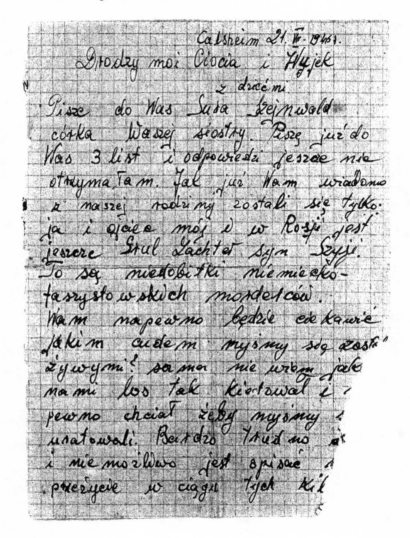

Zeilsheim
July 21, 1946

Dear Aunt and Uncle and Children,

This is Sura Shainwald, your sister's daughter. I am writing the third letter and I have received no answer. I think it is known that from our family there have remained just me and my father...in Russia there is Srulik, son of Shia. These are the remnants from the fascist German murderers. I think you probably want to know with what miracle we have remained alive. I myself do not know what miracle has carried us that we were able to be alive. It is very difficult to write and it is impossible to write about our survival. We never dreamt such a terrible dream... thinking over my memories...I myself do not believe that this is reality. All the time during the survival I thought to myself that perhaps I am in my mind, imprisoned, and that I will become free and I will find everything as it was before the war even though I was definitely aware that this was not the case. When I became free and I came back to my hometown...what and who did I find there? Nobody waited for me...and everything was upside down...debris and graves... (Translator's note: torn/missing section of paper)*...who would believe that I will part with such dear ones and close ones ...that in such a short period of time that I will be separated forever from such close and dear ones...the light has gone out for me...what has remained for me is memories—Yes, my dear ones, I know for certain that with my letter I am bringing to you a lot of pain, but I think that you are ready for these letters. I do not have any happy things to report. Write to me what is happening with you...how you live in such a far-away country...I am finishing my letter and heartfelt regards for everyone, and regards from my father and my husband...*

Yours, Sura

5. Sonia's letter to her relatives in Argentina from the Zeilsheim DP camp. 8/20/1946, original in Russian.

Zeilsheim
August 20, 1946

Dear Uncle and Aunt, and dear kids,

I received your letter for which I am very grateful to you. You cannot imagine my happiness when I received such a tender, heartfelt letter from you. My only relatives, I can report to you that we are alive and healthy, and I wish you health from my very heart. First of all, I want to introduce you to my husband, Isaak Orbuch...Aunt, he's your cousin and now he's my husband. He'll write to you separately. We all live in Zeilsheim camp, as you already know. I will describe for you in greater detail how we got here to the camp and how we survived until our rescue. Of course this will cause you a lot of pain, but then you will come to understand our experience...

In 1942, they began to annihilate all the Jews and in the midst of them, our Luboml. They created a "Ghetto"—and then began to kill all of us. Whoever could, would hide or escape into the woods. Meanwhile we hid ourselves and for two days we were lying in a hiding place, and we almost went out of our minds because 16 people were lying in one small hiding place. Not having any other alternative to save our lives we escaped into the woods. Along the way to Nudyze forest, we lost Aunt Lieberosha. Then when they caught my father and mother, aunt Tziril got away from me and went her own way leaving me all alone. One piece of good fortune is that my parents got away from those scoundrels and came back for me. Then together the three of us escaped into the woods not knowing what would happen to us. We were probably destined to live and therefore it was our good fortune that our Uncle Hersh was left to us—who was without his wife and kids. He was constantly saving us. Everywhere we wandered in the woods, in the mud, with no day, no night, no piece of bread at all—all dirty and cold and fear...We survived like this for a year.

We survived the torments like this for one year. The second year came and the torments were such that there was no way to avoid them in order to save ourselves. There were such days and moments that I thought about poisoning or hanging myself in order to end the torments. But looking at my mother and father who had suffered in order to survive for me, I was obligated to live for them, and they were obligated to live for me. So we suffered until we met up with a Russian partisan group and then we began to live like people. We fought just like the others. They [the partisans] began to treat us like people, to which we had become unaccustomed during all this time. In the first week, we lost our uncle Hersh who went off to a battle and did not return—he wanted to leave for himself his heroism. Praise his glorious memory.

231

We survived the rest of the time in the partisan group until we were liberated. But you see, this still wasn't the end of our grief. To my great misfortune, my mother at the time of our liberation had come down with typhus and died. I am not going to describe for you my experience after the death of the person who was so dear to me. I lost my mother—but not only a mother but also a dear friend. Yes. I couldn't imagine to myself how I could live without mama—me without mama? This wasn't understandable. I wanted to go into one coffin together with mama, but death didn't want to take me, and I got healthier. I became accustomed to misfortune and I began to live without mama, you understand, without mama...

I was left to live only with father—alone on my own without acquaintances, without my close friends and family, in a foreign city, Rovno. I lured myself into thinking that I was going to go home and find everything in order, all like it was before. That happiness, that former vigor, didn't come back; all my close ones were far away from us in the cold, dark earth. Everything had been erased like a dream and it was never coming back. We live and it is impossible to forget this. Always it is standing in front of my eyes. But enough of this unpleasantness...I am sure that you will understand me and that you can already imagine all of this.

Srul Lachhter is already in Poland now. I think that he will be coming to you soon. He married Ruchhela Weisman. She stayed with her brothers. Shneur Vishnitz is now in Palestine. (illegible) now lives 180 kilometers from us. She already has a daughter. It seems to me that I have already written to you about everything.

On this I will end my letter. I'm passing on a "hello" from my father and husband.

Your Sonia

P.S. Excuse me for writing to you in Russian, but it's impossible for me to write in our language right now. I realize that it will be a little hard for you to understand me in this language.

Hello from all of us and to all of you. And a separate hello to uncle Abraham Itzchak.

Your relative who is far away,
Sonia

6. Sonia's letter of May 1947 to her relatives in Argentina from the Zeilsheim DP camp, original in Polish

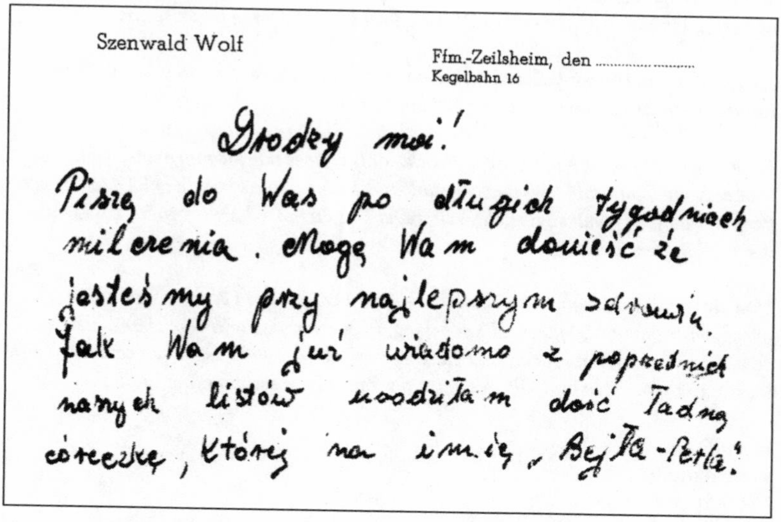
Szenwald Wolf

Ffm.-Zeilsheim, den ....
Kegelbahn 16

Drodzy moi!
Piszę do Was po długich tygodniach milczenia. Mogę Wam donieść że jesteśmy przy najlepszym zdrowiu. Jak Wam już wiadomo z poprzednich naszych listów urodziłam dość ładną córeczkę, której na imię „Bejla-Perla".

Wold Shainwald's letterhead

My Dear Ones!

I am writing to you after long weeks of silence. I can give you the news that we are healthy and I believe that you already know from prior letters that I gave birth to a beautiful daughter and her name is Bejla Perla and the birth was very, very difficult and complicated but I thank God that I came back to health very fast and now we are very happy with our small Bejla...'my mother.' Yes, I have to be satisfied that the name of my beloved mother is still and always to be heard in our abode. Yes, my dear ones, what a pity that you cannot see my little daughter who is already three and a half months old.

It is possible that in the future we will meet. My dear ones, if you think about our coming to you in the future...that is not possible...stop all the endeavors that you have begun concerning that. I know that you would like us to be near you...we cannot do that...because we are thinking not only about the present but also about the future.

Now, about our relatives. Srul Lachter comes to us with his wife and he lives not too far from us. He is not doing too well. His wife is always sick and this is the worst. From Shneur Vishnitz we receive letters and he writes that it is very good for him and he is studying and he also has to work in order to sustain himself. From America he is receiving very little help. And this is probably all I have to write about us.

Please write more about all of you...don't be stingy with letters because "Getting letters from the family brings us all of our happiness."

Now, my dear ones, I have a favor to ask...only if does not inconvenience you. You probably know already how we were able to survive...Some people helped us...these people should be given some help. Whatever I could have done for them I did while I was still in Russia.

Now, it is painful for me that I cannot reciprocate because I cannot send them packages or money. So please, I am asking, in partnership with Abraham, please send a package and appreciation that they were able to help us from a certain death. I write to them often and I do not get a response. I am sending their address:

U.S.S.R.
West Ukraine
Volinsky region
Golovensky district
Village Zabolotye
Farmstead Gromush
Martinetz Tichon Fomovich

And this is the only address I am sending. I do not have any other.

U.S.S.R.
West Ukraine
Volinsky Region
Golovensky district
Village Nudyze
Farmstead Muhavets
Yevdoha Golan

I am asking once more and I am pleading if it is not too difficult to do what I ask; I walk around a long time with this on my mind—that this is the only way to reciprocate to these good people and to thank them. I did not dare before now to ask you.

I end my writing with a bow and an embrace for all of you...Sura

7. Legacy of the Holocaust for the Second Generation

PAUL ORBUCH'S ADDRESS ON YOM HA-SHOAH AT THE OSHER MARIN JCC, SAN RAFAEL, CALIFORNIA, APRIL 19, 2001.

As a child I bore witness to the personal losses in my community.

Growing up, I heard hundreds of stories such as the one just told to you by my mother. You see, almost all of my parents' and grandparents' friends were survivors. Many of them lived in our neighborhood in Queens, New York. Others, we saw at simchas, and during the summers we shared at the bungalow colony in the Catskills. Every simcha became a grand occasion for the reaffirmation of Jewish life, often celebrated by hundreds of close friends.

These people became like family to me, their kids became the cousins I had lost. My mother spoke of the more than sixty close family members she lost. Well, somehow my folks recreated that family feeling for me and for my sister. I felt my family consisted of dozens and dozens of so-called uncles, aunts, and cousins.

I listened to their stories, most often told in Yiddish in my mother's kitchen over a glass of tea, and I think I sometimes surprised people by my interest and understanding of what they were saying to each other. You see, I had the good fortune of growing up with my grandparents so I understood Yiddish. This allowed me to sit quietly and to listen to hundreds of hours of this oral history as these people reminisced about the war, their losses, and their survival experiences. They did so with tears and sometimes with humor.

And almost always there was anger and the refrain, especially meant for any children who may be listening, of "never again..."

At first, I listened with the normal curiosity that all children show about their family's history. My daughter, for instance, is always interested in every detail about my past and so it was with me. But in this case, the subject matter was some of the worst brutality history has ever known.

As the men and women told of their experiences and shared their feelings I began to feel that I was perhaps helping in some small way.

In the popular American culture of the 1950s and 1960s, real men did not eat quiche and they most certainly did not cry in public. But the men in our community often wept in our home; and I bore witness to their heartache.

And so what at first started out as an interest in family stories gradually evolved into the holy task of bearing witness.

And what was the meaning that I chose to make out of this witnessing?

I noticed that nobody ever claimed credit for their survival; and they certainly never considered themselves to be heroes. For them, surviving the Holocaust was accepted as luck, fate...often accompanied by the bitter question: "Why me?"

In time, I came to appreciate the tremendous strength it took for the survivors to carry on after the war. It was so important for them to return to normalcy even in the difficult circumstances of the DP camps. And you heard how they set up schools and cultural centers, how they had kids as soon as they could.

But they did a great deal more than carry on in their new countries; they thrived.

There are thousands of pages on the details of the Holocaust but very little has been said about the heroic rebuilding of lives in the DP camps, and in the new countries to which survivors later immigrated. These people had seen their entire way of life destroyed, yet look what they have recreated in its place.

So the legacy for me has been that although there is, of course, a sadness for our great loss, I have always felt imbued with a sense of grit, perseverance, independence and optimism. Seeing people succeed in life against such great odds has shown me that anything is possible. Striking out on my own in business, travel, or education was second nature to me.

Rabbi Derby, the leader of our Congregation at Kol Shofar, who is traveling this week in Poland with a group of students, talked on Sunday about the duty to be a witness. He then talked about the special nature of being a Jewish witness. He defined this as being a Witness With Hope.

So part of our legacy is this duty to bear witness. And the other part of the legacy is the ability to feel confident and optimistic even in the face of great tragedy.

And I am grateful to our elders for these gifts.

8. Legacy of the Holocaust for the Third Generation

EVA ORBUCH'S ADDRESS ON YOM HA-SHOAH AT THE OSHER MARIN JCC,
SAN RAFAEL, CALIFORNIA, APRIL 15, 2001.

I am here tonight to speak to you from the perspective of the third generation. Each generation has a unique experience and I hope that I can impart a little bit about what it is like to be the third generation. I am the granddaughter of Sonia Orbuch, and over the past 18 years, my grandma has been a vital part of my life. Every week for as long as I can remember, I have gone to her house for Shabbat dinner. It can almost be guaranteed that each week, a new piece of history will come pouring out from the pitcher of her memory, sometimes a delicious sweet drink, and sometimes a bitter liquid. These anecdotes set something loose that she may not have thought about since she was a girl, growing up in her small Polish shtetl, Luboml. The more I hear, the more I am curious. She tells me of her beautiful life there with her beloved extended family of sixty and of their tight-knit Jewish community. She lived a normal life until the Soviets occupied in 1939. Then in 1941, the Germans invaded and the nightmare began. They established a ghetto and in 1942 she escaped into the forests with her parents and uncle. After enduring a horrible winter on their own as fugitives, they managed to join with the Soviet Partisans.

I remember when I was twelve, preparing for my bat mitzvah, and I told my tutor that I understood what my grandmother had gone through. My tutor challenged me on that, and I came to realize that I may never be able to truly understand or feel what my family and millions of others endured. I will only be able to ask questions and grapple with my past. Hopefully, I will be able to use the knowledge I gain to guide me in the future.

As Jews, it is our duty to retell the Passover story year after year, draw out valuable lessons from the Hagadah, and make ourselves feel like we are slaves coming out from the land of Egypt. We can also do this with the Shoah and continue to learn from the stories. There are many families and households of survivors in which the Holocaust has rarely been discussed. I feel fortunate that my past, even with all its pain, is not silence; my past is stories. Sadly, the children of the next generation will not be able to hear first hand stories from Shoah survivors; they will only be able to hear information retold through history books and media sources. In order to make sure the lessons continue to be taught and that our children do not become desensitized to our history, we must personally take it upon ourselves to pass on our stories.

One story in particular that has always stuck with me is when my grandmother and her family spent the long winter of 1942 in the forest. The winter was bitter and cold and they had nothing but their coats to keep them warm. They were extremely depressed, knowing that the Ukrainian nationalists were looking for them and that their lives were in danger. They sat for days, huddled together and hardly speaking. Unexpectedly, a Ukrainian peasant named Tichon came upon them and began to talk with them. When he saw Sonia, then a sixteen-year-old girl, he started to cry saying, "You older people have lived already, but this child, hasn't had the chance to live yet." Tichon himself was very poor and had a big family to feed, but he offered them help. Throughout the next couple of months, he allowed them to eat from his storage of potatoes and he brought them bread and vodka each week, accompanied by his wife and daughter. He also kept them informed on the location of the enemy and was ultimately responsible for arranging a meeting with the Soviet partisan group that my grandmother was soon to join. Every time I hear this story, I am so inspired by the heroic deeds of this man who risked his life and his family to save four Jewish strangers. It is heartening to realize that even though there were such tensions between Jews and Ukrainians, there were good people like Tichon who reached out to help people in need.

When I was in middle school, I began to hear more about my grandmother's involvement with the nearly 30,000 Jewish resistance fighters all over Europe. She had not talked a lot about this before, and suddenly a whole world opened up for me. Many people today are still unaware that there were Jewish resistance fighters during the Holocaust, but I think it is so powerful and important for us to know that some Jews actually did have the opportunity to fight back. I feel an immense amount of pride each time I think about my grandmother living in the forest, learning how to care for wounded soldiers, guarding the camp at night, and going on missions to sabotage Nazi trains. I know she wasn't doing it to be a hero, she was doing it to survive, and I just wish that every Jew could have had the opportunity to fight back like she did. When I hear about my grandma's life in the partisans, I feel so connected to her and can relate because she was the age that I am now. I can hardly say that she was having a normal teenage life, but this seventeen-year-old girl was experiencing some things that I can certainly relate to now. She was going through the beginning phases of romance, leaving her protected family cocoon, and growing out of her childhood shyness. But there are other ways in which our lives are so completely contrasted. She was carrying hand grenades on missions, and I am now fretting over college choices. But I try to do the impossible: to walk in her shoes and try to understand the frame of mind of a teenage girl who is fighting because it is her only choice, and fighting because she wants revenge for her sixty relatives who were killed and for the fact that her life and freedom were being denied her for the sole reason that she was Jewish. And now, when I sit with her today, I also try to put myself in her shoes, as a woman who has come so far and has so many loving people around her, yet at times, feels utterly alone and empty, for she is among the very few left from her entire first grade class.

My grandmother and many of the people who resisted in their own ways were
Jewish teens who made a difference in their time, and now in the twenty-first
century, I want to do my own part. When I began to learn more about my grandma's
unexpected role as a resistance fighter, I knew that I needed to carry on this spirit.
Although she was working for survival and I am working because I have the luxury
to do so, I still feel that we share some of the same lessons.

I want to share my favorite quote from my grandma: "From all sides there was
shooting. I didn't even bend down my head; I wasn't worried that I would get killed.
If I was going to get killed, I was going to get killed as a fighter, not because I am a
Jew." To me, this means that it was important that she not let herself be defined
by the oppressors. I realize that the immediate result did not matter to her; she felt
inherent satisfaction in being able to resist and struggle for her cause. I know that
there were millions of acts of resistance that we don't even know about. Today, I am
catching onto the inherently joyous nature of fighting for a just cause and for Tikkun
Olam, just as my grandmother did years ago.

Rabbi Menachem Mendel, the Kotsker rebbe said, "There is nothing so whole as a
broken heart." In certain ways, we are the broken-hearted people. I think we can
take this knowledge of the wholeness of our broken hearts to feel the suffering of
other people. A few weeks ago, I organized a panel at my school to raise awareness
about the Darfur Genocide. We were fortunate enough to have a Sudanese refugee
who is now living in the Bay Area come and speak to us. Mr. Ibrahim spoke of his
home village and how he was one of the only survivors out of two hundred friends
and family members. I could feel the desperation, frustration, and urgency in his
voice, as he pleaded with us to do something. As I listened to this man, watching
tears run down his face, I felt an intense connection to him, and it was almost as if
we had the same story, for this too had happened to my grandmother. He could have
been a man who had escaped from a concentration camp, attempting to convey to
the world the urgency of what was happening to his people in Europe. That moment
was when I truly realized that suffering cannot be compared, it is only shared. A
mother who loses a child in Sudan is the same as a mother losing a child in Israel or
in the Palestinian territories or in Poland.

Martin Luther King, Jr. said that, "Injustice anywhere is a threat to justice
everywhere." We as Jews have gone through so much hardship and it is our
responsibility to take action as early as possible against other injustices in the
world. In the words of Abraham Joshua Heschel, "The opposite of good is not evil.
The opposite of good is indifference. In a free society where terrible wrongs exist,
some are guilty but all are responsible." I know that during the Holocaust, most
of the world acted as spectators, refusing to become too involved and stand up to
the Nazis. I cannot bear the thought that the world would again stand by while

people are being murdered for no reason. The Holocaust has given us a Jewish eye about how to approach other genocides, and the way I see is it that their suffering is our suffering. Sometimes I wonder how my life would be different if I had all of those lost relatives with me today. We live in such a shaky world right now, where there are people extreme enough to deny the fact that the Holocaust even occurred. We owe it to our elders to keep the promise of "never again" and speak out against any injustice or discrimination that we see in the world. I know that as I head off to college, I have the daunting task of fighting for justice, keeping my history alive, defending Israel, watching out for anti-Semitism, and so many more things. But I know that I will have strength and inspiration simply by thinking of my grandmother, the strongest woman I know. I also want to say that I am filled with admiration for the way all of the survivors have shown us how to rebuild and how to be resilient and strong after tremendous loss.

Growing up, I never understood exactly why grandparents, especially Jewish ones, were so in love with their grandchildren. I always thought it was just how grandparents are and are supposed to be. But I have come to realize that perhaps they love us so much because to them, we represent the ultimate victory. The fact that we are alive and here, living day to day, signifies the Jewish success. We as a people are no longer just trying to survive—we are creating and thriving.

9. Official notification from Yad Vashem, Jerusalem, designating Tichon and Fedora Martynetz as "Righteous Among the Nations," 10/15/01.

YAD VASHEM   יד ושם

The Holocaust Martyrs' and Heroes' Remembrance Authority   רשות הזיכרון לשואה ולגבורה

Jerusalem, 15 October 2001

RE: **MARTYNETZ TIKHON & FEDORA – UKRAINE (9371)**

We are pleased to announce that the above persons were awarded the title of "Righteous Among the Nations", for help rendered to Jewish persons during the period of the Holocaust.

A medal and certificate of honor will be mailed to the Israeli consulate/embassy listed below, which will organize a ceremony in their honor. Their names will also soon be added on the Righteous Honor Wall at Yad Vashem.

Copies of this letter are being mailed to the honorees, to persons who have submitted testimonies, and other interested parties.

Dr. Mordecai Paldiel
Director, Dept. for the Righteous

cc: Mrs. Sonia Orbuch
     Ambassador Anna Azari, Embassy of Israel – Kiev

P.O.B. 3477, JERUSALEM 91034, TEL. 02-6443400 FAX. 02-6443443   02-6443443 פקס. 02-6443400 טל. 91034 ירושלים, 3477 ת.ד.
www.yadvashem.org.il